# Bring out yr

# HEARTS
# ARE HERE!

## Gorgie Aggro 1981 - 1986

**A TERRACE BANTER PUBLICATION**

*To those who helped me put this book together*

Bring Out Your Riot Gear - Hearts Are Here! (Pbk)

© C.S. Ferguson, 1999

ISBN 0 9535920 0 6

Published by Terrace Banter, Scotland
Printed by Victoria Press, England

Respect to the Edinburgh gangs of the '80s - Leith Mods, Danderhall Beat Boys, Central Skins, East Side Skins, Gillie Mods, Broomie Skins, Fernie Mods, Central Mods, Bar-Ox, Casual Soccer Firm, Gorgie Skins, Capital City Service, Blackley's Baby Crew, Orchard Football Trendies, Gracemount Baby Crew, Hyvots Dressers, Saughton Chosen Few, Muirhouse Casual Firm, Wester Hailes Casual Crew, Murrayfield Tufty Club, and all the others that I have forgotten.

A Terrace Banter publication from
S.T. Publishing
P.O. Box 12, Lockerbie, Dumfriesshire. DG11 3BW. Scotland.

"The behaviour of the Hearts support was
appalling.  There was a hard core group of
some 300 youths who were not in the
slightest interested in football . . .
they were more concerned with causing
trouble on the terracing . . . "

Allan Herron, Sunday Mail,1982

# Three Cheers For The Red White And Blue

from a novel by Gavin Anderson,
author of *Casual*

There's about 50 of us making our way up to the Olympic Stadium . . . A fuckin' UEFA Cup quarter final . . . I cannae really take it in, but we're here all right, in Munich. The CSF in Hitler's heartlands. 50 good boys, that's all we need for they sausage eating cunts.

I look around . . . all the separate mobs have come together under the CSF banner. Wester Hailes, Gorgie, Muirhouse, Livi, Kirkcaldy . . . everyone is represented. 1-0 up from the first leg, you're no exactly gonna miss this, are you? Fuckin' Bayern Munich in the quarters, everyone that matters is over here.

It's been a laugh up till now, but as we approach the ground, and a few of their boys are around, it gets more serious. Yesterday was all about having a good sesh. Some of the boys went up to Dachau to see the concentration camp . . . no my idea of a laugh that, so I stayed in the boozer. That's until a couple of boys from Morningside way done the till over. Fuckin' Morningside . . . you'd think they'd know better, they cunts. Anyway, the Old Bill turn up, and took one of the boys away which was a bit of a dampener. Fuckin' stupid thing to do anyway.

Apart from that the only trouble we'd had was with some Hearts scarfers . . . fuckin' idiots. All dressed up like Christmas Trees, shaking hands with all the Krauts. Wankers, the lot of them. It's enough to give Hearts a bad name. Anyway, we're walking up the main drag, just past a couple of bars, when one of they idiots clocks the London accent from one of the Chelsea boys who's with us. There's only three of them over, but to the Christmas Trees, it's like Bannockburn all over again. Only this time they didnae win.

Some cunt shouted - English bastards!!

*Then it's their favourite . . . the one they copied off the Celtic fans . . . they've no even got the brains to be fuckin' original - It's magic you know, Jam Tarts and casuals don't go!*

*When we stopped, a few of them looked a bit uneasy, like they didnae want any trouble. Well they should've kept their fuckin' mouths shut. They know the score with us. Some of them would maybe have saw us in action in Vienna after the game when about 30 of us scattered over 200 of them . . . practising on the Plastic Germans before doing the real thing.*

*Although saying that, looking at some of the wankers outside this boozer, they probably wouldnae have been there. Fuckin' glory hunters the lot of them.*

*Anyway, right away some of them are easing themselves back into the pub, but there's always a few lairy wankers who think they're Charlie Big Time. Always has been at Hearts . . . but before, they had something to back it up with. This new lot are tossers. Most of the decent boys from the old Shed joined the ranks of the casuals about three years back, although unfortunately not all of them stayed with Hearts, or they grew out of the rucking altogether. Moved on to gardening or dragging the kids around Homebase every Saturday afternoon.*

*Now we're confronted with what was left . . . cunts too clueless to cope with the fashions of the casuals, or too attached to their cheapo £3 Hearts scarves to discard them. That, and the new breed trying to make a name for themselves.*

*So, we've stopped in the middle of the road, and fanned out as we fronted them up. None of us was really into it. We didnae come all the way to Germany to fight a bunch of wankers from Edinburgh, but we're no going to turn the other cheek from that shower . . . that'd be a victory to them.*

*They outnumber us . . . there's only about 20 of us here . . . the rest are still singing about Spurs in Dachau, and there's probably around 50 Christmas Trees still outside the pub. Cunts in makes of jeans that you've never heard of before. Ali Brothers finest fashions . . . there's no need for it. Replica shirts and scarves to a man . . . fuckin' diddy men. Fat little cunts with moustaches . . . blokes that would cut you up in their locals back home, and are quite willing to have a scrap with us, but no with the Germans. Gotta keep the good reputation of the Scots intact. Ambassadors for their country and all that Tartan* for the foreigners . . . at school it was all the *Rule Britannia* stuff, in the tabloids it's all about keeping ahead of Johnny Foreigner. We are raised as cannon fodder, to fight their next war for them. Secretly the ruling classes love it when we kick off abroad. They love watching the whole of Europe run in fear when the Union Jack appears. It makes them feel safe . . . there's nothing to worry about with the working class always ready to fight their battles for them. Obviously the scarfers get the same shit as us, and deep down they think like us, like all British people . . . but some people are warriors, and others aren't.

All it took was for one of them to throw a bottle. They'd given it all the - *Come on ya casual bastards!* - then the bottle flew at us.

That was it. We steamed them . . . a few of them stood and had it with us . . . which was fair play, but the rest of them are trying to get into the *Guinness Book Of Records* by trying to beat the record for the amount of people able to get through a two foot wide doorway at the same time. It would've been laughable if it hadnae been so embarrassing. That was it then. We let the cowards get away with it whereas the decent lads got a kicking.

Anyway, that was this afternoon. It's getting dark now as we start to walk across the park towards the huge concrete arena that Bayern play in. It's right on top now for us. There's Turks everywhere standing alongside their German hosts. So much for them hating each other. It doesnae look as if they want to shake hands with us, which suits us fine. We're here for Britain, not to make friends. Remind they cunts who the masters of Europe really are, as the Upstarts sang - *HEADS HELD HIGH . . . FIGHTING ALL THE WAY. . . FOR THE RED WHITE AND BLUE!*

A few of the Penicuik lads who are at the front of the firm are shouting instructions to stick together. Keep it tight. Giving confidence down the ranks. There's no real top boys today, just people geeing each other up, and looking after the Baby Crew lads who have come over. The strength of the unit is what it's all about. There may be about 50 of us here, but there's only one unit, and that one unit wasn't backing down from anyone tonight.

They're all around us now . . . trying to get in between us to split us up. Not fancying their chances in a straightener, they *want to beat up small groups of stragglers as usual. We're not letting it happen though . . . we stay tight, stay focused. Everyone is watching each other's backs. They should put management trainees in situations like this. Let them learn what real team work is all about.*

*The Germans know the score, they know the rules, they're not amateurs, like so many of the other Europeans, but we're not scared. Tense yes. Scared no. If this was back home . . . in Leith, or up in Aberdeen, or in Glasgow, you'd be a lot more worried. Outnumbered about three to one in the middle of a park, surrounded, with no Old Bill around to give you an escort, would not have been a good proposition, but over here we don't give a fuck. Germans are wankers. No moral fibre. We're confident of an away win off the pitch . . . anything our forefathers can do, we can do better. You know no one's going to run because there's nowhere to run to. So there's no worries about steaming in . . . we're a unit not a gang of individuals.*

*Something's happening up front. The roar goes up and some of us surge forward. I look to my right and see a Turk coming at me with a blade. My whole body jars as the right hook I've thrown connects with his chin and he goes down. The blood is pounding in my head as I aim a trainer at his head. One of the Baby Crew bends over and grabs the guy's knife and cuts him down the cheek. The squealing of the Turk is lost as the designer trainers stamp him into unconsciousness.*

*They're backing off . . . still giving it the big one, but shocked at what's happened to their mate. They thought that we'd run, and they don't have a clue what to do now that we're taking it to them. Up at the front, a Hearts boy has been slashed on the arm, but about three of them have been stabbed. They've backed right off.*

*We're buoyant . . . we know we can't be touched. Britannia, our guiding spirit, is showing us the way forward in the same way as she guided the men of 1941 and '45. Going through my head is the knowledge that no matter what they throw at us, we can't be beaten.*

*- Come on Hearts! They're fuckin nothing - scatter the cunts.*

*Commands from up front and we wade in again. Like an atom exploding, we charge at them in all directions. They can't believe it. Their resistance is weaker now. They're firing their flares, but still we keep going. We're not playing by their rules.*

*Some of them are taking really bad beatings as the lads take advantage of the lack of police. They expected a bit of bravado, and a bit of posturing, not a massacre.*

*No mess, no fuss, just pure impact. The Union Jack conquers yet again.*

*A few of us have CS gas sprays, and I'm running past Germans rolling around on the grass, hands over their eyes, screaming with blindness, as the Baby Crew give them a dose of pure Sheffield steel.*

*They're running in all directions . . . panic on their faces as I lash out when they run past me. All the Hearts boys are laughing like maniacs wide eyed, pupils dilated, breathing heavily, high on the adrenalin buzz. We're losing it big time now . . . it's a fuckin' massacre.*

*Fuck the game . . . what happens here is what it's all about. The Krauts knew all about the English, but they didn't know what to expect from us. They thought we were just going to be a bunch of kilted pished up Jakeys who want to shake their hands while exposing ourselves to their women . . . in true ambassadorial style of course . . . but they didn't expect this.*

*They're gutted. They're slowly learning their place just like the rest of Europe will. It doesnae matter from what part of this small island we come from. England, Scotland, Wales, they know we'll scatter them cos we have what they don't. Pride.*

*There's sirens in the distance now, but they're fast approaching. We're nearly at the ground, the crowd's getting thicker. The Germans numbers have swollen, but all that means is that more of them are running from us as we push forward . . . No retreat, no surrender . . . FIGHTING ALL THE WAY FOR THE RED, WHITE AND BLUE.*

# Introduction

Most Hearts fans will be puzzled at the choice of period that I have decided to write about. After all, we were hardly a force to be reckoned with in season '81-'82, and despite the near success in '85-'86, we had still not won anything. But this book doesn't have anything to do with the performance of the players on the park, and it certainly has nothing to do with the modern, sterile image of the game today. It's all about a time of youth cults, going to the games with your mates, excitement, and most of all, having a laugh.

Those were the years just before the "nouveau" football fans started to invade our game, and just before the families started to turn the atmosphere inside the grounds into something more akin to a Saturday afternoon matinee at the cinema than a passionate game of football.

Football crowds had always been an integral part of the game, rather than just spectators. You were part of the team - the so called twelfth man. Basically, it was all about participating. Now, it's all about spectating, providing an audience, no different to a cinema or theatre audience. The Taylor Report may have outlawed terracing, but the new fans, the trendy bandwagon jumpers, have outlawed passion. The loudest they shout is when they are telling one of the true fans to "sit down!".

In August, 81, me and my mates started following Hearts regularly, home and away, because it was exciting. Let's face it, there couldn't have been any other reason because Hearts were shite and in the First Division, after being relegated the previous season from the Premier League. Everywhere we went there was the same hardcore group of fans who travelled around the shitholes of Scottish football, supporting the lads.

With a loyal travelling support of around 1,500 to 2,500, we were soon to gain a reputation as the most notorious fans in Scotland. At the time it didn't seem much, it was just a laugh, but in hindsight, it's easy to see why we caused so many problems. The Hearts support had gained a bad reputation in the mid Seventies, and alongside the Old Firm, we were every police force's nightmare. We had led a yo-yo existence for the last few seasons - too good for the First and not good enough for the Premier - so it was important to the fans to do the business off the pitch while the team inevitably let us down on it. After being relegated in season '80-'81, finishing the season bottom of the league with a mere 18 points (only two points a win in those days), it was up to us, the fans, to do the business in the First Division. Teach the minnows a lesson and show the Premier League what they were missing. That was the aim and that's what happened.

There will probably be a lot of people reading this who have started following the Hearts since 1986 and who will be disgusted at the behaviour portrayed in these pages. Well, tough! This is written for the loyal hardcore who, despite the depths the team had sunk to, never turned their back on the club. You know who you are.

I was just a kid, still at school in 1981, so obviously I was not one of the hard men or main faces. I am only writing this account as I saw it from being on the edges most of the times and occasionally in the thick of things. Hopefully, if one of the main characters around at the time reads this, it may inspire him to write a definitive account himself.

Lastly, the reason I stopped at 1986 is twofold. Firstly, I began to lose a bit of interest, a bit of the enthusiasm died that day at Dens Park, although I still watched Hearts every chance I got. Secondly, with football discarding its working class roots, it doesn't seem as important now. The game has changed, the crowd has changed, and I don't really feel the same sense of belonging that I did before. There isn't the same camaraderie anymore, and that was the main reason that me and thousands of other young men from the housing estates of Britain were willing to spend their last penny on following their team. Better that than spending it in some shooting gallery in Leith anyway.


C.S. Ferguson, 1999.

# Chapter One

The summer of '81 had seen Britain in flames as the reality of Thatcherite policies drove home. Although Edinburgh hadn't really experienced the same level of violence as the cities in England, there had been a few copycat incidents in Niddrie, and more notably, Muirhouse. Here, the streets around the Terror Towers of Martello Court became a battlefield as locals clashed with the police in a night of street battles, petrol bombs, and burning barricades. However, the anger soon subsided and depression set in once more. Depression that in the following years would see Edinburgh with one of the worst smack problems in Britain.

Growing up in central Edinburgh, it would've been easy to go down that route, because, let's face it, there didn't seem to be much to look forward to. Unlike now, Scotland then was pretty unfashionable, so much so that the Tories wanted to close it down. In the words of The Clash, there was a "white riot" waiting to happen, and the forgotten generation was venting its anger and frustration at football games at this time.

August, 1981, and the youth of Edinburgh was divided. Not by religion as in Glasgow, or even by football due to Hearts and Hibs being in different divisions for the last two seasons, but by youth cults. Every weekend since late 1979, gangs of mods and skinheads had gathered in the city centre and more often than not there was some kind of kick off somewhere along the line. Most of my mates at the time were mods, although we knew quite a few skinheads as well, and most of us had been mods since 1979 / 1980, and were getting a bit bored by then. To be honest, the majority of the time the mods took second prize in the fighting stakes on a Saturday afternoon anyway, so that was another reason for a change of scenery.

Although there was a lot of skinheads at Hearts matches, there were no problems with them, football being the uniting force. So on the 29th of August, 1981, three of us went through to Dunfermline on the service bus for the first league game of the season. The game was nothing special, the sub-standard Hearts team playing out a 1 -1 draw with the equally poor opposition, but to three teenagers at their first away game on their own, it was excellent! You felt like you were part of an invading army.

When we got to the ground all you could see were gangs of Hearts fans standing around drinking, having a laugh. Once inside the ground it soon became obvious that about half of the 4,500 crowd was in the visitors end, and the atmosphere was exhilarating, probably due to the fact that the vast majority of the Hearts fans at the time were in their teens or early twenties. It was a totally young support and basically all lads.

For most of the game we didn't even look at the field of play, we were too busy staring out the home fans on the other side of the fence. Eventually, the staring and chanting turned to coins and gobbing as we all swayed down towards the fence. The police, who were ignoring the locals, moved into our end to make a few arrests and instantly people steamed into them, forcing them to make a tactical retreat minus their hats.

After the match, in the street outside the ground, it was all off. Dunfermline, who had been mouthing off all game, felt they should make some sort of stand and Hearts tore into them. About 50% of our fans were up for it and the Fifers soon took to their heels. Walking back towards the town centre felt superb with all the cars having to stop for us, what with us in complete control of the Queen's highways. The Gorgie Boys are in town! First class!

Just before reaching the town centre, the main group of Hearts fans cut across the park to go back to the station, but me and my two mates had to get back to the bus stop for our transport back to Edinburgh. Suddenly, there was less and less maroon and white around us and out of nowhere there was a lot more black and white who weren't best amused. A few older Hearts fans who were still around got griefed up, but luckily our youthfulness ensured that we got back to the bus stop in one piece.

Ten minutes to wait for the bus, and just as we were beginning to relax again, a little mob of Dunfermline about the same age as us approached. There were about half a dozen of them and it looked on top for a while. Everyone stopped speaking and they just stood around us, staring. It was a nightmare, although it wasn't getting a kicking that really worried me. It was more what my mum's reaction would be if I came home with a few bruises! It would probably have put a stop to my going away just as it started.

Those ten minutes felt more like an hour as we waited for the bus, but it came at last, and only as we got on did they start mouthing off at us and gobbing. I couldn't believe it. What a bunch of wankers. They could have slapped us while they had ample opportunity. They had the numbers, but out on the street they didn't fancy it. I suppose that's the benefit of following a team with a reputation. The downside showed itself later that season when whole towns started turning out for us. People that had never supported Queen of The South, Ayr United, Clydebank and the like, suddenly popped up when we were playing. Basically, if you followed Hearts away regularly at that time, you would probably end up in some sort of trouble, somewhere along the line, whether you liked it or not.

* * *

Even in 1981, it mattered to us what we wore to football, especially to away games. As mentioned before, most of the Hearts fans were skinheads or just herberts, but there was one item of clothing that was common to all of us - the green flight jacket. The standard look for herberts was flight jackets with Razzy jeans and ski jumpers, usually rounded off with either Adidas Kicks or, on occasion, Sambas. Not forgetting the obligatory wedge. The skinheads would wear them with burgundy Fred Perrys, army greens, and Docs, while we would have button down shirts, sta-prest, and desert boots, although we started wearing Oxford brogues as the violence escalated.

Everyone wore scarves then. Plain maroon and white bar scarves looked the best and that's what most of the lads wore. Harrington's were also popular at the football, with the maroon ones not surprisingly being most popular with the Hearts. However, they were more a start of the season and end of the season thing because they didn't keep you too warm - the flight jacket, or occasionally a parka, was essential for the winter months. Some of the older skinheads wore West Ham scarves, a combination of the similarity in colours and the fact that top skinhead band, the Cockney Rejects, were well known West Ham hooligans. In fact, the Hearts were the first in Scotland to sing their own version of the *Bubbles* song -

> *I'm forever blowing bubbles,*
> *Pretty bubbles in the air,*
> *They fly so high, they reach the sky,*
> *And like the Hibs, they fade and die.*
> *Celtic's always running, Rangers running too,*

*We're the Gorgie Bootboys*
*And we're running after you!*

This was a direct result of the West Ham influence on the skinheads at the time. However, later during the casual days, the Hearts mob had connections with Portsmouth and Darlington.

There were also quite a few punks in our support at that time as well, most notably Wattie of Edinburgh punk band, The Exploited. Many a time during a terrace row you would see the mohican hairstyle in the thick of things. Despite his infamous *Fuck The Mods* song, there was never any problems between us and Wattie (thankfully).

Over on the other side of Edinburgh, the Hibs support was roughly made up of the same type of fans. They had a skinhead support that was drawn from the East and South Side of Edinburgh, although they didn't seem to have many punks. The Hibs Skins were largely from the well known East Side and Central Skinhead gangs, while Hearts attracted the skinheads from the estates on the west of the city. Most notably the Broomhouse Skinheads.

Hearts also drew a large hooligan support from the new town of Livingston which eventually caused a few problems in the following season with a lot of in fighting. The Livi Punks and Skins were a respected mob, and as mods we had come across them many a time in town - and I've still got the bruises to prove it! A Saturday afternoon in the summer of '81 had seen the mods and skinheads in Edinburgh join together to have it with Livingston. They had arrived firmed up and tooled up, and it was right on top for Edinburgh who were all split up. Eventually, we got it together outside the YMCA that used to be in St Andrew Square as Livingston were coming towards us. At that time, builders were converting an old shop on the corner of St Andrews Square and Princes Street into Top Man, and there were a lot of scaffolding poles and bolts to hand. Armed with them, the Edinburgh mob tore into the Livi, who eventually backed off into Princes Street Gardens, where battling broke out everywhere. It was mental when you think of it. Scaffolding bolts flying during a 100 a side gang fight in Edinburgh's main shopping street on a Saturday afternoon. Crazy!

With incidents like this occurring, maybe it wasn't too surprising that there was also problems at the football with Livi. And the following week, it was also back to normal between the mods and the skinheads in the city.

* * *

The week after the Dunfermline game saw us at home to Kilmarnock. Although there was only about 5,000 at that match, the atmosphere was far better than it is today. The lads all stood at the corner of the Shed at that time, and most of the singing and most of the violence came from this section of the crowd. Kilmarnock were one of the bigger teams that we would play that season and they brought about 300 fans. Not exactly a huge travelling support by today's standards, but this was the Scottish First Division.

Away fans were put in the Gorgie Road End terracing if the police expected a fair number. Some teams only got the section of the Enclosure towards the School End, or both ends. Kilmarnock were in the Enclosure, and their celebrations after going 1-0 up were greeted by a chant of the infamous, "You're gonna get your fuckin' heads kicked in!" (in fact almost every team who scored at Tynecastle at that time was serenaded with this).

The game finished 1-0 to Killie, and they did indeed get their fuckin' heads kicked in. The Shed had emptied with about three minutes to go, and gathered outside the Enclosure at full time. As the 300 Killie fans came out, Hearts steamed in. This was before organised firms and basically anyone was fair game. The police moved in, got a hold of the away fans, and escorted them to their buses which were parked at Chesser. The Kilmarnock fans looked well scared, and at the time I did feel a bit guilty, but years later when I witnessed them at Meadowbank terrorising young Bankies fans, I came to the conclusion that they deserved all they got that day.

17

# Chapter Two

The next few home games were all pretty low key due to the fact that neither Hamilton, Clydebank or Dumbarton brought many with them. Crowds were dreadful, even dropping below 4,000 for the visits of Hamilton and Dumbarton. During that run of home games, there had been a couple of away games at Falkirk and at Ayr United. Unfortunately, I wasn't able to get to either of them, but after hearing about the offs at both those games, I made sure that I visited both towns later on in the season (every team played each other four times a season).

Following on from the Dumbarton match, we were away at Queens Park and that is one weird experience. Hampden at that time held 88,000, and being in a crowd of only 2,450 is a bit strange. We went through by train for this game, getting into Glasgow early in the morning. There were a couple of good shops in Glasgow selling off the peg mod gear at the time, and the most memorable thing about that trip was the fact that I bought a tonic suit from a shop down on the Trongate. It was well smart, brown two tone, and it wasn't something that many mods in Edinburgh had. The game certainly wasn't memorable - Hearts hit rock bottom that day with a 1-0 defeat by what was literally a bunch of amateurs. How was I going to live that down at school?

The next big away day was Queen Of The South on the 10th of October, and that is a story in its own light. In fact the whole weekend was mad. On the Friday night before the game, a lot of the mods from Edinburgh went down to a disco at the Brunton Hall in Musselburgh. It was mayhem. All the little East Lothian towns had teamed up - Tranent, Prestonpans, Musselburgh, etc., because they knew we were coming. There were about 30 Edinburgh mods in there and also a few girls with us. We hadn't been looking for trouble - if we had, we wouldn't have taken the girls - but trouble is what we got. The mods were mostly from Gilmerton, Leith, and the city centre which on any other occasion may have caused problems, but this time we stuck together. We had to.

We'd been in this place for about haft an hour, with dirty looks flying about, but nothing too heavy. Then one of the Edinburgh mods got jumped in the bogs, and it all kicked off as we piled into a group of blokes who had done our mate. The next thing, all hell broke out with glasses, tables, chairs, the lot, coming flying at us. As

18

we retreated to the door, I was left defending myself by waving a chair leg that I used to keep in my parka, hoping to connect with someone. Once we got out in the street, we managed to stand and stop them getting out the door after us. As soon as we heard the sirens, we all scattered and most of us managed to jump on a bus that was passing. The next time we went down there, there wouldn't be any girls with us.

The following day I met my mates at Haymarket first thing in the morning and got on the infamous Gorgie Sons Of William Hearts supporters bus to Dumfries. This bus had a hard reputation, and we were well out of our league. We just sat at the front and tried to look inconspicuous all the way down there.

We arrived about 11.30am and almost immediately it kicked off. The bus dropped us off at a market in the town centre and soon Hearts fans were charging through the stalls, clashing with the locals. The locals were well up for it on account of a Hearts fan having stabbed a Queen's supporter the last time the teams had played in 1978, and it looked like every man and his dog had turned out for us. Eventually, the older lads went to various pubs in the town centre, which every so often would erupt into a scene from the Wild West, leaving us younger ones to fend for ourselves on the streets. For the next hour or so, we were getting chased everywhere until more Hearts fans arrived by bus and train and we started to get the upper hand.

Eventually, it was time to go down to the ground. We paid into the covered terracing behind the goal which was halved down the middle to create a home and an away end. When I say halved, I don't mean by fencing or anything like that. No, there was only about three or four coppers trying to keep the opposing supporters apart. Pretty standard for Scottish games back then in the lower divisions.

The game started with the groups staring each other out and chanting. Then the stones, bottles, and coins started flying about. They piled down towards us giving it, "We are the Queen Of, the Queen Of The South!" It sounded mad.

Hearts steamed in, and for a couple of minutes, it was going mental. All the youngsters from both sides were down at the front and we were having our own little war when more police piled into restore some calm and cart a few people away, mostly Hearts fans. As half-time approached, and rumours swept the terraces that a Hearts fan had been stabbed in the earlier exchanges, it started to kick off again, but it was mostly missiles this time. As the players were leaving the field, a few of us ran across the pitch into the old Cow Shed, along the side of the park, but the locals in there didn't want to know.

As the second half started, the situation on the terraces calmed down and for about the first time in the match we were able to actually watch the game and cheer Hearts on to a deserved 2-1 victory. Which, considering Queens got relegated at the end of the season, wasn't exactly a convincing result.

After the match, there were a few scuffles around the ground, but we made our way back to the bus in one piece for the journey home. Funnily enough, there wasn't as many people going home as there had been on the way out of Edinburgh!

The following week we were at home to Raith Rovers where over 5,000 saw us win 2-1. But it was the match the following week that everyone was looking forward to. A top of the table clash away at Motherwell attracted a healthy crowd of around 7,500 who witnessed an entertaining 2-2 draw. We had a huge support that day with around 3,000 in the away end. There was the usual surging at the segregation fence and some scuffles with the police. However, the Hearts fans mostly got behind the team and gave them excellent vocal support for 90 minutes, totally drowning out the home fans. This was the game where the 'Well Well, fuck your Well, fuck your Motherwell!' chant started.

On the way back to the buses after the match, a charge had the home fans backing off, although they got a bit of revenge by blocking our buses on the road out of town and ambushing us. Everyone was crouching on the floor with seats up at the windows, as the bricks came through to the sound of breaking glass. It was a cold, draughty, and uncomfortable journey back to Edinburgh.

After the decent result at Motherwell, Hearts brought us back down to earth with a home defeat against the mighty East Stirlingshire. Ironically, a fairly decent crowd of 5,000 attended what was a totally dire display. This was even worse than the Queens Park match at Hampden, and it was this type of inconsistency that would cost Hearts dearly at the end of the season.

The inconsistent results continued through November, December and into the New Year, but we were amazingly still up there challenging at the top of the table. But after a 1-1 draw at home to Queens Park, Hearts eventually sacked manager, Tony Ford, and appointed Alex MacDonald as caretaker manager. This was when we started to turn the corner, but at the time few would have realised it.

The Cup didn't last long - after beating East Stirling 4-1 at Tynecastle in the Third Round, we crashed out at home in the next round by the only goal of the game to the mighty Forfar. 5,600 turned out for that one, but even the hardcore were beginning to lose patience. Many thought that this was the lowest point in the history of our club. Journalist and Hearts fan, John Fairgreave, even suggested that it would be better to fold the club and turn Tynecastle into a car park rather than carry on with the embarrassment.

It was after this match that the club gave the manager's job properly to Alex MacDonald, who continued in the post as player manager. The fans were not impressed though, and only 2,397 turned up on the following Wednesday to see us beat Queen Of The South 4-1, and I can honestly say that I was one of them.

The following Saturday, we were away at Ayr United, a game which was always good for a ruck and this was no exception. Again, there was a decent away following (about 800) in a crowd of just under 3,000, and we provided superb backing from the covered shed behind the away goal as Hearts coasted to a 3-0 win.

The layout of the ground appears to invite trouble because after the game you have to come out into a lane at the back of the main stand and walk right up to the home end to get to where the buses are parked. At that time, it was all loose gravel on this walkway and as we came behind the stand, the Ayr United mob at the top of the path came charging down chucking stones at us. Hearts charged back and once again it was all off, with running battles back to the bus. An excellent end to an excellent day.

\* \* \*

The battles between mods and skinheads in Edinburgh had reached their peak by now, with punch ups almost every week in the city centre. Most of them were fairly minor, but there were the odd one or two that were massive. The best example of this occurred in February, 1982, when about 200 youths were involved in battles along Rose Street. There were about 120 mods that day, and around 80 punks and skinheads, and when they met up in the precinct, it went mental. It was a great day because it was one of the few times that the mods had the upper hand, and running the skinheads onto Princes Street, giving it large with the "WE ARE THE

MODS!" chant, felt brilliant. It was like you were ten feet tall as the entire Saturday afternoon shopping crowd stood and watched.

However, for all that, it wasn't as good a crack as it used to be in town on a Saturday, and I'd rather have been at the football. The camaraderie was better and the excitement ten times better simply because everyone we played was up for it when we visited their town. It was the away days that done it. Just the chance to get away from Edinburgh, your parents, and the boredom of every day life for those few hours was worth every penny, but to couple that with the feeling of being part of an invading army was immense.

Arriving at those towns, with the police out in force, looking worried, edgy, all for us, gave you a sense of power that you didn't normally have as a spotty teenager. The mod scene was beginning to wane at that time anyway, although there was no way that I'd pack it in since I was waiting to get my scooter next year and there was the small matter of a Jam gig at the Playhouse coming up. Plus the fact that there was nothing else around at the time. Mainstream fashion was a cross between New Romantic and soul boy, neither of which appealed, so mod it was for the time being. Also, being a mod meant modettes, which was as good a reason as any to stay with the cult.

The thing with Musselburgh hadn't been forgotten, and there had been groups of Edinburgh going down fairly regular since the big off last autumn. I had only been once more when there must have been about 50 or 60 of us, including a few friendly skinheads. We almost filled a double decker bus, but this time there were no girls. We kicked it off literally within minutes of arriving, and this time we done a bit better. One of the locals got cut, and a few other people were injured by flying chairs and the like. The police arrived very quickly, and we were soon all on the bus back to the city centre with the police tailing us all the way. I didn't really think it would be wise to go down there again.

# Chapter Three

After the last few games had produced some encouraging results (except for a 2-1 reverse at St Johnstone), we decided to make the 25 mile trip to Falkirk on the 6th of March. The crowd was only listed as 2,500, but around 800 to a thousand were visiting fans. Most of us were crammed in the shed along the side of the pitch, right next to the temporary netting that served as a segregation fence. Despite the backing from the fans, Hearts being Hearts lost 3-1, and as a result some of the worst crowd violence of the season kicked off.

Inside the ground, it all started to turn nasty at the netting, as the Hearts fans surged repeatedly towards it in an attempt to get at the Falkirk who'd been giving it loads throughout the match. The police moved in and basically got a kicking when they tried to make arrests. It was crazy, the whole of our support just seemed to be up for it. Even after the police had calmed things down a bit and had pushed both sides back from the fence, coins and assorted debris rained down on them (and the linesman) for most of the match.

At the final whistle, the fans were in an ugly mood and only a heavy police presence at the front of the terracing prevented a full scale pitch invasion. When we got out on the street, it was total mayhem. We had to get back to Falkirk Grahamston station along with around 200 other Hearts fans and we were running riot. Falkirk weren't exactly innocent in this either, and it was going back and forward along the street for about 15 to 20 minutes and that's no exaggeration. As well as the actual toe to toe stuff, there were bottles, bricks and other missiles to look out for. In all my time following Hearts since then, that has to be the best street battle that I have ever witnessed. Pure adrenalin, and if you could market it, you would make a fortune. In fact, it's a pity all the smackheads in Edinburgh then couldn't have experienced that rush. It would have made a far more effective substitute than methadone.

After that riot, we had a week to recover before another visit to Dumfries. This time, two of us travelled with The Manor bus, which although having a few boys on it, was a lot safer than the Gorgie Sons Of William. We arrived in Dumfries about one o'clock in the afternoon, and this time there were a few younger Hearts lads hanging around so it wasn't as on top as the previous game. There were a few scuffles before the match that I saw, but it was quite low key. Once in the ground however, it was like a re-run of the last time. We had the same bit of the covered terrace, but this time there was substantially more police on duty to keep the fans under control. It looked like it would do the trick until a Queen's fan unfurled either a Hibs or a Celtic scarf. Hearts went mad and steamed straight through the police lines. This time the locals weren't as up for it, and instead legged it over the pitch into the Cow Shed. The game was delayed for a few minutes as the police cleared the pitch. Another great day out that was capped by a superb 5-1 Hearts victory.

I missed a few games after that, and my next one was St Johnstone at home on the 3rd of April. We ran out easy 3-0 winners, but it didn't prevent the 500 or so Perth fans getting ambushed on their way back to the coaches. Hearts losing the police by hiding down the lane at the side of the brewery and using spotters to tell us when to come out.

Football was to take a back seat a few days later on Tuesday, the 6th of April, when it was off to see The Jam at the Playhouse. About ten of us went from school and we saw them play a blinder. I'd seen them once before a couple of years previously, but I was probably too young to appreciate them fully then. This time was different. Of the 3,000 crowd, I would say that about 2,000 were mods. All the Edinburgh mod gangs were out in force from Leith, Gillie, Corrie & District, Niddrie, and so on, together with mods from all over Scotland. The mod girls were there in force as well, and we wasted no time in getting to know a mob of them from Motherwell.

The Jam were awesome, as they promoted their forthcoming album, *The Gift*, and also ripped through their back catalogue. The Playhouse bouncers stood helpless as Weller urged everyone to come down the front. There wasn't much they could do with hundreds of pilled up mods steaming past them. Those that tried to restore order got slapped.

After the gig, we mobbed up in the foyer of The Playhouse and about 500 of us left together. The 30 or so skinheads who had been hanging about over the road pissed off pretty sharpish when we made a move towards them (can't say I blame them). Everyone was walking in the road, chanting "We are the mods!", with the traffic wisely stopping to let us past. One twat biker didn't stop though and scattered us going up Leith Street. We gave chase and, unluckily for him, he got stopped at the lights outside the old GPO. Needless to say, he took a severe one, with his bike also getting trashed. After that, it was a case of seeing the Motherwell girls back to the station, via a doorway in West Register Street. Very Quadrophenia.

The following Monday was the Easter Bank Holiday, so a few of us mobbed up outside St James's Centre then got the bus down to Portobello. Altogether there was about 200 mods down there, and about 50 skinheads. There were a few rucks in the fun fair, and we got chased across the beach, but the only slap I took that day was from my mum who had heard all about it on the radio by the time I got home.

The following Wednesday, it was away at Clydebank. Hearts won 5-1 in front of a bumper crowd of 960! Despite the paltry attendance, there were about 400 Hearts fans there, and we managed to bring the game to a halt as we kicked it in the ground. There were a few Celtic fans in the Bankies end, and the Loyalist songs were coming thick and fast from the Hearts fans in response. It was all fairly standard stuff, but when a Celtic fan crossed himself in front of the Hearts end, the violence moved up a level. He got a slapping, and as we started to smash up the wooden bench seating on the terracing, the police moved in and initially took a hiding. The game was held up while all this was going on, and soon the police were calling for reinforcements from Glasgow. *Sunday Mail* journalist, Alan Herron, wrote in his column the following Sunday that we weren't welcome in the Premier League and that the behaviour of the Hearts support was appalling. All great stuff, and it's a cutting that was treasured and shown proudly around my school.

It seems hard to comprehend that so much trouble could be caused by such a small crowd. There were only 400 of us there, the loyal fans, and this happened. Never let it be said that hooligans are not true fans. We were the best fans Hearts had then - in fact we were the only fans they had then. Another thing of note was the Loyalist chants. Hearts were down to their core support and almost every song that night was sectarian. Take note all the people who now ask, 'What have Hearts got to do with all that?' Like it or not, it's part of supporting Hearts.

Saturday the 24th saw a return to Dunfermline. This time, I travelled on a supporters bus - fuck all that hanging about at bus stops. We got to the ground just before the kick off, so I don't know if anything occurred beforehand. We ran out 2-1 winners, but surprise surprise, it kicked off on the terraces again, with an advertising hoarding at the front of the Hearts end collapsing and a well known Hearts fan from Niddrie breaking his arm in the process. Afterwards,

Dunfermline came round to the buses, and it went for a couple of minutes before Hearts ran them back.

Despite the inconsistencies earlier on in the season, we had strung a few good results together since Doddie had taken over, and we were all quite hopeful of promotion. Motherwell were streets ahead and had the championship sewn up, and it was between ourselves and Kilmarnock for the runners-up spot. We looked to have two easy home games next, against East Stirlingshire and Dumbarton. The first match went according to plan as we won 2-0, but disaster struck the following week.

5-2! 5-2! How the fuck can you get beat 5-2 at home by Dumbarton?! It's a scoreline that I still find hard to believe. Despite all the disasters earlier on in the season with Queens Park, East Stirling, and the like, this still came as a shock. Not surprisingly, the paltry Dumbarton support went home wishing they had never bothered to come through. To make matters worse, Kilmarnock had won 5-1 and we would be without two of our most experienced players for the following week's match . . . away at Kilmarnock.

10,000 turned up at Rugby Park the following week, about 4,000 of whom had travelled from Edinburgh. Again, we jumped on a supporters bus at Haymarket and got into the ground without any problems. Most of the Hearts support was crammed into half of the covered terrace along the side. The game was hard, and you could almost taste the tension. Tempers boiled over on the pitch with a player from each side getting sent off after an off the ball incident, and tempers boiled over on the terraces. At the mesh segregation, coins were flying through from both sides, and the police snatch squads moved into the away end to drag people out. Throughout the first half, there was a steady procession of Hearts fans being carted off around the side of the pitch. The police got a slap on one of the occasions that they were making arrests, and after that it got a bit dodgy at the fence. They swamped the area and were just nicking anyone. At half-time, quite a few Hearts fans (us included) moved round to the terracing behind the goal. The match finished 0-0, and really the only interesting bit on the pitch was when an old man came out of the Kilmarnock end and attacked Henry Smith!

So, it was all on the last weekend of the season. We had a one point advantage and a superior goal difference of four, but we were at home to champions, Motherwell, and Kilmarnock were playing already relegated Queen of the South. The situation certainly caught the imagination, and the kick off at our match was delayed by five minutes to let a crowd of just under 15,000 in (where were they for the rest of the season?!).

There was a sizeable Motherwell support of about a thousand in the Gorgie Road terrace, and the atmosphere was electric. However, with the crowd behind them, Hearts decided to get an attack of the nerves and on the half hour mark we were silenced as Motherwell went 1-0 up. As the away fans celebrated, the Shed suddenly found their voice, and responded with, "You're gonna get your fuckin' heads kicked in!"

It was still 1-0 to the Well at the interval.

Just after half-time, with the news coming through that Kilmarnock were 5-0 up at Queen Of The South, a riot kicked off in the Shed. A fight was staged to entice the police onto the terraces, and once they arrived, everyone waded in. The police took a hammering and three of them spent a night in hospital with head injuries. Seven fans were arrested and numerous others were ejected as reinforcements arrived. Hearts chairman, Wallace Mercer, came over to appeal to us to calm down, but he was ignored and pelted with coins and a few bottles.

Just two goals would have been enough for Hearts to gain promotion, but we never looked liked scoring. With about five minutes left and Kilmarnock having won 6-0, Hearts fans were leaving in their droves to go round to the Gorgie Road end. By the time the Motherwell fans came out, there were literally thousands of us milling around. The Motherwell fans got charged all the way along to their buses, the police just about managing to save them from a complete hiding. Time and time again, the mounties charged us, but we just kept steaming back. There were so many of us that the police couldn't really control it. A few Motherwell fans who were trying to go the opposite way back to the station didn't have an escort and they got absolutely leathered.

This trouble occurred out of pure frustration. There we were, the famous Heart Of Midlothian, doomed to another year in Division One. A lot was said after the riot, all the usual stuff about dragging the club's name through the mud, a disgrace to football, blah, blah, blah. Fuck them. They were the disgrace. Years and years of mismanagement by the various boards was the disgrace. The second rate managers, the second rate - no that's giving credit where it's not deserved, the fourth rate players were the real disgrace. For years, the people running and representing Heart Of Midlothian Football Club didn't give a fuck about us, so why should we care about them? We were Hearts, not them. It was our club, not there's, and they had almost killed it. And they had the cheek to call us a disgrace! Well, fuck them, fuck them all.

# Chapter Four

The summer months. Every football fan's nightmare. To tell you the truth, I felt so low after the Motherwell result that for once I was glad of the break. There was a lot of talk that Hearts would have to go part-time to survive another season in Division One, but luckily Mercer decided to take a gamble, meaning that next season would be do or die. At the time, I wasn't too sure if that was the right idea as we hadn't exactly set the heather on fire last season, but at least it avoided the humiliation of part-time football.

After a couple of weeks with the hump, I started to look forward to the World Cup in Spain. Scotland, England and Northern Ireland had all qualified so national interest was at an all time high. Of course, with the recent British victory in the Falklands, there was also the chance that there would be stacks of trouble. Whilst on the subject of The Falkland Islands, I'll always remember the day that the news broke that the Argies had invaded. I turned on the radio and heard this solemn voice explaining that the Argentinian Army had invaded The Falkland Islands, and that we were now at war with them. My first reaction was, "Shit, some of the islands on the west coast of Scotland have been invaded," and there was huge relief when I looked at the position of the islands in my atlas.

Anyway, the build up to the World Cup started in earnest with the release of the songs. I can't remember the Irish effort, but the Scottish one made me cringe. *We Have A Dream*, what a load of crap. England led the way in the songs stakes with, in my opinion, the best ever football record, *This Time (We'll Get It Right)*. Despite all the excitement of the build up, the Finals were the usual anti-climax, with Scotland failing heroically (again) to qualify for the second phase in our last group match against the Russians. Same story, different setting. Even the England fans behaved fairly well, so no excitement there either. I did chuckle at the 'Malvinas Inglaterra!" chants though.

Most weekends in the summer were spent hanging around in town with the mods. Every Saturday we would gather around the art gallery, and depending on the numbers, something might happen. There were also a few days out to Glasgow shopping, but it could be a bit on top there. They had a mob called the Glasgow Combat Skins, and it was bad enough being a mod when you bumped into them, but coming from Edinburgh was the icing on the cake. As a result, we were on our toes a few times through there.

For a few weeks we had a laugh, but by the start of July you were just counting the weekends to the start of the season. Being a football fan is strange. No matter how crap your team were the previous season, you are always full of optimism for the start of the new season.

Basically, it was music that got you through the summer months. Anthems that summer were two Jam tracks. *A Town Called Malice*, which had went to number one in January, and *Just Who Is The Five O'Clock Hero*, released in June. We were all bang into The Jam's latest (and best) album, *The Gift*. A more soulful sound, it was probably the most "mod" out of all their albums.

We were also beginning to get into Northern Soul around this time, going down the same road as a previous generation of Edinburgh teenagers who made the pilgrimage to The Casino Club in Wigan during the Seventies. Youth club discos all over Edinburgh were rocking to the sounds of rare '60s and '70s soul that summer. The sounds from the '79 revival were also still very popular - *It's A Mod Mod World* by Squire, *My World* by Secret Affair, *Millions Like Us* by Purple Hearts, and *Maybe Tomorrow* by The Chords, being the big favourites. We also started following Edinburgh band, The Questions, who had got in with Weller and had supported The Jam. The Questions at the Corrie Youth Club was a particularly memorable gig.

I started listening to some of the Oi! stuff around then as well (on the quiet, obviously). Since many of the songs were about life on the terraces, I could relate to them straight away. Anthems such as Cock Sparrer's *Trouble On The Terraces* still gets me going today. The classic line, "It's all part of the game, it adds to the atmosphere!" sums up the lifestyle perfectly. The Cockney Rejects were also big favourites with *War On The Terraces* and *We Are The Firm*. In general though, the Oi! stuff was just good sing-a-long tunes, no match in my view for the mod sounds, but enjoyable nevertheless. It was music for all of us. *ACAB* by the 4-Skins summing up the attitude of a generation. If you don't know what it stands for, you were obviously never there. All you need to do nowadays to see how much impact that song had is to look at the knuckles of 30 something males all over Britain, and the tell tale four Indian ink dots gives the game away.

Clothes wise, all us younger mods were copying Weller. Polka dot or Paisley pattern button downs were all the rage that summer. Bought mail order from Carnaby Street, they looked the business with white sta-press and a pair of Jam bowling shoes. Cycling shirts were also big, as the mod look got away from the suits and became more relaxed. The look at football the following season would be much the same as the previous year, with Harringtons at the start, and flight jackets and parkas in the winter. Although crew neck woollen knitwear was worn on dry winter days with a button down underneath. The start of a casual look at Hearts?

So, after a family holiday in England it was back to Edinburgh for the start of August and a friendly against Leeds United at Tynecastle to get you raring to go for the new season.

# Chapter Five

By the start of a new season, you're so desperate to get started again that even the meaningless friendlies look attractive. This season I made the effort to get to two pre-season matches, home to Leeds United and away at Hibs in the Tom Hart Memorial. Although both technically friendly matches, the atmosphere at them was anything but.

At the Leeds match, they turned up mob handed. They had about 200-300 fans, of which at least 50-60 were members of their Service Crew. What we found strange at the time was the fact that riot many of them were wearing colours. In fact, although we didn't know it at the time, they were the first casuals that we had seen at Tynecastle. Pringles, trainers, the early casual look.

During the game, there was the usual abuse coming out from the Shed, with plenty coming back from them. Although we won 1-0, a decent sized firm of us waited at the back of the enclosure for them to come out. When they did, they were well up for it, and it went mad for a bit before the police sorted it. To tell you the truth, from where I was standing, it looked as if they got the better of us. They were well game, and brought a taster of organised football violence to Edinburgh.

Two days after that match we went to Easter Road on a Monday night for the only Edinburgh derby of the season. It was a benefit match for the Hibs chairman, Tom Hart, who had recently died, and we were playing for a Memorial Shield. 10,000 turned up, and the crowd was probably split evenly. We were well up for the game as Hibs were a league above us and they had got the better of us in our recent league and Cup meetings. The game itself was crap, although the noise from both sets of fans created a great atmosphere, more than the match deserved. It looked like it was going to end 0-0 when right on the final whistle Hibs scored to win 1-0. Immediately, thousands of Hearts fans surged towards the exits. People were losing it big time. We knew it was going to go pretty major, but nothing prepared us for what followed.

When you leave Easter Road, it's easy for the police to segregate you from the main body of home fans by closing roads to keep the rival fans apart. Although this segregation worked pretty effectively again (there were a few charges past the barriers, but the police lines held), there was so much pent up anger that it was going to be let out somehow. As we turned into Easter Road, the riot started in general. There were over a thousand of us rampaging up the road, smashing fuck out of anything that got in our way. Cars were trashed, shop and house windows put in. It was mental.

The police, who were woefully outnumbered, tried to intervene and they got hammered. They were forced to retreat and basically watch what was going on with little hope of stopping it. Once in London Road, everyone was charging towards Leith Walk where you normally bumped into Hibs fans. However, I think they must have heard us coming because by the time we got there, they had disappeared.

The situation was beginning to calm, and we were all standing outside St James's Centre wondering what to do next when a number 7 bus got stuck in traffic in Leith Street. On the top deck at the back there were about 15-20 Hibs fans who had a tricolour hanging out the back window emergency exit as they gave it the big one. A bit silly as we're standing next to the bushes, with loads of stones to hand. During what followed, literally every window in the top deck was smashed along with some in the lower deck as we tried to get onto the bus. The police arrived in time to prevent this, and the mob split in two, some going up Leith Street and the rest of us going around the side of the car park into St Andrews Square bus station. The Hibs fans waiting at the bus stands got hammered as about 300 of us ran through, eventually meeting up with the rest of the mob on Princes Street.

The adrenalin and energy had returned, and the shop windows on Princes Street started to go in, including about seven of Jenners, the top people's store in Edinburgh. This was during the Edinburgh festival, and the town was full of tourists who were a bit bemused to say the least by what was going on. However, the Japs seemed to enjoy it judging by the amount of photos they took.

Eventually the police arrived in force with dogs, horses, and no doubt every other animal they could muster, and my last memories of that night are of getting chased up The Mound by an alsation. The following day on the radio and in the papers, the police said it was the worst night they had ever experienced due to football, and certainly I've never seen anything since that could top that. Although the actual fighting was minimal, it was a totally mad night. A top buzz.

For the rest of the week, the newspapers really went to town on us, calling for Hearts fans to be banned from travelling. All of the incidents that had occurred last season were aired again, and everyone was building up our League Cup match on Saturday to be potentially violent. Not that it needed any building up. We were away at Motherwell!

# Chapter Six

So, the first competitive match of the season takes us back to Motherwell in the League Cup, and bearing in mind what happened the previous season, trouble was always on the cards. We got through there by train, arriving at around 1.30-2.00ish. There had already been battles in the pubs in town and the place was crawling with police when we arrived.

As usual at Motherwell, we stood on the side terrace up against the segregation fence, and the usual insults were traded with the home fans who were very mouthy. However, they didn't seem to have much to say when Hearts celebrated a goal by Derek O'Connor by kicking off a riot with the police on the terracing which resulted in several arrests. The game ended in a 2-1 defeat, and at the final whistle hundreds of Hearts fans made their way around to the home end exits and trouble broke out. Unfortunately for us, the vast majority of this mob then jumped onto the supporters buses, leaving us to make our own way back to the station which was a bit hairy.

The next game in the League Cup group was against Forfar on the Wednesday night at home. A bumper crowd of 1,900 turned up to see us win 2-1 in a game that was instantly forgettable. On the Saturday, it was a bit more convincing, and more evidence that maybe we had turned the corner as we crushed Clyde 7-1 at Shawfield. Quite a few of us went to this match, basically because it was a new ground for us. There were about 2,000 there, mostly Hearts fans, and we managed to generate some atmosphere in this greyhound-cum-speedway stadium. You're miles away from the pitch, there were no home fans to speak of, so it was just as well the lads did the business on the park.

After this win, and a 2-0 midweek victory at Forfar, we had the return against Motherwell at Tynecastle, and over 9,000 saw us get our revenge for the previous season with a 1-0 win. We were basically through to the quarter finals now, which was confirmed by a 3-0 win over Clyde in midweek.

The quarter final drew us away at St Mirren in the first leg, which believe it or not was a huge match for us then. Over 5,500 were there including an excellent midweek travelling support of about 2,000 who played up a bit after the match which ended 1-1. We couldn't wait for the second leg at the end of September.

* * *

The Jam had announced another concert in Edinburgh. This time it was at Ingliston, the week after we played St Mirren at home. This gave the Edinburgh mod scene a little boost as everyone began to look forward to it and plans were made to mob up. So, the next couple of Saturdays saw me hanging out in town, where there was quite a sizeable mod presence. There were, on occasions, in excess of 100 of us, and it was a laugh for a couple of weeks giving the police the runaround.

Around this time a few of us started attending Uptowns Disco in the South Side on a Saturday night. It was originally an over 18s place, but due to trouble they had started catering for the 16-20 year old age group, and although it was soft drinks only it was open from 10pm to 2am. Mad Hatters Disco on The Royal Mile had an under 18s night from 6.30-9.30pm, so from about midday until two o'clock the following morning, you were out with your mates, which was pretty cool when you were a kid.

Mad Hatters could get a bit on top at times, as there wasn't any door policy, and as a result the place was often full of skinheads. Punch ups were regular because the DJ had a habit of playing Secret Affair, followed by the Angelic Upstarts, followed by The Specials. Sometimes we had the numbers and done them, but the vast majority of the time it was well on top for us, and the only thing that saved me on various occasions was that I knew a friendly skin girl who was going out with one of the main skinheads in Edinburgh at that time.

I can't actually think of many mods who wanted to go there, but unfortunately it was a favourite hangout for the modettes so it was a question of face. The nights at Mad Hatters continued well into the following spring, but we eventually knocked it on the head after two or three weeks when the mod numbers dropped to single figures as the skinheads topped the 100 mark.

Uptowns was a far better proposition. A door policy meant no skinheads, and the late opening had all the top mods in there. The main gangs to hang out there were the Leith, Niddrie, and Gillie Mods, and although there was the occasional off between Leith and Niddrie, it was largely peaceful. Uptowns was more of a mainstream disco as regards to music policy, but we outnumbered the normal punters and it was always regarded as a mod hangout. Occasionally there were some skinheads up for a row afterwards, although by

2am their numbers were depleted and it wasn't too much of a problem, even if it was still unwise to leave early on your own. Ironically, one of the few big offs with skinheads outside Uptowns occurred one Saturday evening when my dad had been out with his mates, and had decided to hang around to give me a lift home. He had parked just along the road from the club, and a charge by us as we came out had the skins backing off. Unfortunately, they decided to make a stand just where my dad was parked, and I'll always remember everyone battling around his car as he looked on. When the fight had moved along the road a bit, and I jumped into the car, all he said was, "Had a good night?!" Bizarre!

Sunday night was also a crucial time at Uptowns as they had a Northern Soul club then, and once again it was well attended by mods. However, with school the next day, my attendance at this required a certain degree of negotiation, and unfortunately I only had two superb nights there. The Uptowns era ended towards the end of the year when the club burnt down. Another nail in the coffin of the Edinburgh mod scene, coinciding as it did with the news that The Jam were calling it a day.

* * *

Back to the football. Before the big game with St Mirren we had three important league games against Ayr United at home and St Johnstone and Falkirk away. I didn't make it to the first two games, but I heard that there was fun and games at St Johnstone on the Wednesday night. There was a bit of a heavy atmosphere on the terraces of Muirton Park that night with Hearts' reputation ensuring that the local mob were out in force. Calling themselves the Perth Pack, they were a largely skinhead gang and a good couple of hundred of them charged Hearts on their way back to the buses after the match. The Hearts fans stood and had it, with the police arriving to spoil everyone's fun as usual.

Falkirk away the following Saturday was basically a watered down version of the previous season's match at Brockville. As with the last time, we went through on the train and after the match there were more running battles on the way back to the station. Although nothing like as bad as in March. Inside the ground, the coppers had it a bit more sussed and prevented a repeat of the terrace battle. Hearts drew all those games 1-1 which was a bit worrying in a season which was definitely make or break.

At last, the big night came with the second leg against St Mirren. Nowadays, it's hard to imagine how much excitement there was around this game, but believe you me, everyone was up for this one. A great crowd of over 12,000 turned up and the atmosphere was electrifying long before the kick off. There's something about a night match that brings out the best in a crowd and the hairs were standing up on the back of the neck that night. Roared on from the start, Hearts swept into the lead when MacDonald scored midway through the first half, causing Tynecastle to erupt. Even a St Mirren equaliser didn't calm the crowd, and when Pettigrew put us 2-1 up with about 12 minutes left the place went mental. Despite a desperate attempt by St Mirren to salvage the match, we held out. The atmosphere that night showed what the Hearts crowd could achieve. We may have been criticised by all the media for the violence then, but no one could criticise the backing that we gave the club that night.

You couldn't underestimate how important this game was for us. Apart from the obvious money making potential of reaching the semis, it showed that we were able to match what was then a decent Premier League side. Teams like St Mirren, Dundee Utd, Aberdeen, and Dundee, the so called new firm of Scottish football, had replaced us and Hibs in the late '70s and early '80s as credible opposition for the Old Firm's traditional domination of Scottish football, and this was proof that we were on the way back. Defeats by teams like St Mirren had been the reason why we were relegated, and this success gave us cause for optimism again. And of course a great Tynecastle night had to be rounded off by encouraging the visitors to get back to their coaches a bit quicker than they intended.

So, Hearts in the semi-finals and the draw certainly brought a smile to the faces of everyone connected with Hearts, from the treasurer to the thugs. Rangers would do nicely thank you very much!

\* \* \*

The next big event on the calendar was The Jam at Ingliston and it was to prove one of the best nights of my life. There were special buses being run by Eastern Scottish from St Andrew Square bus station to the gig and when me and my mates arrived there around 4.30pm the place was a sea of green parkas. It was excellent just walking about, meeting old mates that you hadn't seen for ages, and catching the eye of the numerous modettes. Despite a night of jumping about in a crowd of 9,000 ahead, I had a few layers on . . . tonic suit, Ben Sherman and tie, topped off with a parka. A bit plastic a few people will no doubt say, but I was still at school and this was 1982. Being mods for us was more about the gang culture, speed, and music, rather than the snobbishness that ruled the scene later on. We had more in common with the gang mods of the Sixties who became skinheads than we did with the art school set who became hippies. Jumping about, giving it large with "We are the mods!", chatting up birds, having a runaround with the skins and the Old Bill, popping black and whites, blues at soul nights, and basically just "belonging" meant more to us than middle class mugs wearing original '60s gear, trying to look cool. As the saying goes, if you have to try to look cool, then chances are you're not.

When we got to Ingliston, there was already a huge queue, but the main group of Edinburgh mods walked to the front and pushed in. A few slaps were dealt out to anyone who objected. Once inside, the atmosphere was superb. Everyone seemed to be a mod and even those that weren't joined in the "We are the mods!" chant. Just before The Jam came out, the DJ played *The Kids Are Alright* by The Who, and the place went mad. Suddenly, in the middle of us were two leather jacketed punks, one of whom had a "I hate mods" target badge on. Whether he was mad or just totally stupid we never knew - they both had to be stretchered out before any questions could be asked.

The Jam as usual played a blinding set and definitely sent the crowd home happy, unaware that in a couple of months time the Scottish mods would have one last big gathering at the Glasgow Apollo to say farewell to the best band to come out of Britain.

Once we got back to the city centre, literally hundreds of us had a mooch around for an hour or so, but the proposed clash with the skinheads never materialised and everyone began to drift off home.

That night at Ingliston was probably the pinnacle of my time as a mod. It's impossible to describe the unity felt at that gig. It's like a huge tribe coming together, knowing that the end was in sight. It will be one of the nights from my teenage years that stays with me forever.

* * *

Two days after The Jam gig it was back at Tynecastle for a 4-1 win over Clydebank. But a trip to Kirkcaldy on the following Saturday for the match against Raith Rovers brought us back down to earth as Hearts lost 1 -0. A shit game. It was only livened up with a brief ruck with the coppers at the back of the Shed behind the away end goal. The walk back to Kirkcaldy station was pretty uneventful. However, looking forward to a night at Uptowns kept the spirits high.

Finally, the Rangers game arrived. We were away at Ibrox in the first leg and the press were building it up on the crowd violence front. Rangers gave us the whole of the Broomloan Stand (6,000), and in a Hearts programme for a preceding game, there was a plea for good behaviour from the club and Strathclyde Police, together with a recommended route for us to take which would ensure complete segregation around the ground. I wonder why?!

With it being a midweek game, we jumped on a supporters bus at Haymarket and got through to Ibrox no problem. This was the biggest away game that I'd been to without my old man and the adrenalin was working overtime as we approached the ground. The police segregation worked well and the only Rangers fans that I saw were around a souvenir stall that we had stopped at to buy some Ulster badges. I do believe though that there was a bit of trouble involving other fans before the game, but we never saw anything.

Going into Ibrox was a pretty awesome experience. Although I had attended a game between Rangers and Hearts in the Seventies with my dad before the ground was modernised, the size of the place took my breath away and the noise that we were making was unbelievable. Even drowning out the 16,000 Rangers fans in the 22,000 crowd (this was before the David Murray era when it wasn't unknown for the Rangers home support to drop below 10,000).

Although Hearts played well, the 2-0 scoreline in favour of the home side was probably a fair reflection of the game. I knew that it was unlikely that we would turn a 2-0 deficit around in the second leg, but I was still pleased with the team's performance. We hadn't got hammered and that was the main thing. It was more evidence that we could more than hold our own with the Premier Division teams. Also the backing that the 6,000 of us gave the team was immense, so there was also a genuine feeling of pride that night.

However, with such a large travelling support, elements were always going to play up a bit and extensive damage was done to the toilets in the Broomloan Stand and a few seats came out at the end. Obviously, after the match it was a lot harder for the police to keep the rival fans apart and there were a few clashes on the way back to the buses. Unfortunately, not all of them going our way!

The next two league matches were a bit of a disaster. A 1-1 draw away at Partick Thistle, and a 4-2 home defeat by Airdrie. I didn't make it to either of those matches, but I made sure I was at Tynecastle along with 19,000 others on Wednesday, the 10th of November, for the second leg against Rangers. There were about 5,000 away fans and the atmosphere was red hot. Hearts were never going to overturn the deficit from the first leg, but I couldn't care less. We were all looking forward to what we knew would happen at the final whistle. All I wanted was that Hearts wouldn't be disgraced, and a brave performance by the lads meant we ran Rangers close with a 2-1 defeat.

After the game, the Shed Boys walked out the McLeod Street exit and up onto Gorgie Road. As we met with the Rangers fans walking towards the station, a huge charge by hundreds of Hearts fans had them running full tilt back along Gorgie Road. One of their beer bellies stood and fronted all of us on his own. At first it seemed that people were conveniently ignoring him as they ran past to chase fleeing Rangers fans. But eventually someone punched him, and once one person had done it loads of people steamed in. The geezer was hard as fuck and well game, but eventually he went down and took a severe kicking. He deserved better than that for having the bottle to stand.

The next major incident was outside the chippy on Gorgie Road, just past the away end. A Rangers fan walked out at the wrong time, just as Hearts were charging past. A few people grabbed him and he ended up going through the chip shop window. After that the police arrived in numbers and started pushing us back along the road. As we were going past a bus that was stuck in traffic, someone noticed a bloke with a Rangers scarf sitting at the back seat next to the emergency exit. The next thing, the exit is opened and the bloke is getting dragged out and hammered. The police tried to intervene, but everyone was losing it big style now, and there were people trying to pull coppers off their horses. It was totally insane. There was another clash between the fans at Haymarket Station, Rangers having a pop this time and doing a bit better. The police charged us again and we legged it along Shandwick Place and into Princes Street. Once there, it was like a repeat of the Tom Hart Memorial match as the windows went in, with Jenners again being the main target. I'll always remember a Hearts fan running along the road with a portable TV in his arms then seeing him jump into a taxi before departing the scene! It was sheer madness.

The papers the next day were full of it, and the following Hearts programme had a right go as it described the 'Maroon Morons' who once again dragged the club's name through the mud. There were also the usual letters in the programme and the newspapers from fans who claimed that the trouble made them ashamed to be Hearts fans. Big deal. It was probably their first match of the season anyway. Glory hunters.

*  *  *

I think now is the time to say a bit about the team that we had then. Although we weren't aware of it at the time, this was the nucleus of the side that would see Hearts rise to the top again. Alex MacDonald didn't really have enough time to prevent us from failing to get promotion the previous season. There had already been too many dropped points by the time he was appointed. In fact, it has often been said that it was the best thing that could've happened to Hearts, having another season at the lower level, because it gave us time to build a team properly. The feeling was that if we had gone up we would have come straight back down again.

At the time, we had a few good young players in Dave Bowman, Gary McKay, and John Robertson. The last two of course went on to form the nucleus of the Hearts team for many years. However, they were relatively inexperienced so MacDonald set about bringing in older more experienced pros to help the youngsters, and the close season saw the arrival of ex-Rangers stalwart, Sandy Jardine, who was to become joint player manager with Alex MacDonald. Then, in September, another ex-Ranger came to Tynecastle, Willie 'Bud' Johnston. Now, everyone knew about the drugs thing in Argentina in '78 when Johnston got sent home, and everyone knew about his bad boy image, but what is forgotten a lot of the time was how skilful a player he was. Even at the twilight of his career he was turning it on, and the Hearts fans loved him. Soon the famous "We've got Willie Willie Johnston on the wing . . . " chant was echoing around Tynecastle. Only a few years earlier The Shed had been screaming abuse at him as he deliberately studded a grounded Hearts player while appearing for Rangers. Such is the fickleness of football fans. Everyone loves a hard man, as long as he's playing for you.

# Chapter Seven

Hearts had a good run in the league up to Christmas with the only dropped points being at Dumbarton where we drew 1-1. A definite improvement on last season's 5-2 defeat! I went to all those matches and although there was some sort of incident at almost all of them, it was pretty small scale.

To tell you the truth, the main event at that time for me made football take a bit of a back seat. The Jam announced that they would split up after the release of a final single, *Beat Surrender*, which went straight to number one and would become the anthem of the nation's youth over the Christmas period. However, there was one last chance to say farewell, since a final UK tour (fittingly called the Beat Surrender Tour) included a night at the Glasgow Apollo on the 25th of November.

It was a must for every mod worth his salt in Edinburgh, and we managed to get tickets and seats on a coach from Sound Centre (now Ripping Records) on the South Bridge. It was an immense gig, and very emotional as the mod gangs from all over Scotland came together for one last time to pay their respects to what John Weller, Paul's dad, said was the "best fuckin' band in the world" as he announced their imminent appearance on stage. It was the night that Scotland's greatest youth cult started to die. Things would never be quite the same again.

Although the gig was excellent, the sadness prevented it from topping Ingliston. Also the fact that we were surrounded by Weegies didn't help. There were a few scuffles outside the Apollo with their boneheads, but we weren't interested. It was a Glasgow thing and had nothing to do with us so we went straight back to the bus.

The Jam eventually called it a day on Saturday the 11th of December when they played their final gig in Brighton (where else?). As Paulo Hewitt says in the booklet of the recent box set, "Brighton is a mod town and The Jam were, to all intents and purposes, a mod band." After the gig, the band and a few of the London faces stood silently on Brighton Pier to mark the end of an era. The mod revival, 1978 - 1982.

\* \* \*

Monday, the 27th of December, away at Ayr United, and an ideal opportunity to escape the TV and work off the excesses of a family Christmas. We got the Manor Hearts bus down there and again cheered Hearts on to a 3-0 win. It was good to see that the police had learned their lesson after the match last season. NOT! Full time saw both sets of fans leaving the ground at the same time and clashing behind the stand outside the home end. If anything, the trouble was worse this season and seemed to go on for longer. So much for the season of goodwill to all men!

A New Year's Day game against St Johnstone didn't seem quite right, although this was a table topper and vitally important to both sides. The part-time supporters were out in force again as 14,500 turned out to see us win 1-0. Despite the celebrations and hangovers, we still had enough energy to run St Johnstone all the way back to their buses.

The next big event was the Scottish Cup Third Round and the draw couldn't have been better for the regular travelling support - Queen Of The South away! Apparently, on the week leading up to the game there were reports on Border TV about extra police from Carlisle being drafted into the town as they prepared for World War Three. After the events of the previous season, the police decided to segregate us on the open terracing behind the goal opposite the end of the ground that we were normally in. They even put up temporary fencing. They were shitting it big time. They knew we were coming and they reckoned they could control it.

We got the Manor Bus down there arriving about two hours before kick-off. As usual, it was going off around the town and in the pubs, and although Hearts were doing alright, it wasn't always going our way. Around ten of us had it with a few of their younger lads on the road back to the ground, but we ended up on our toes. Just before kick-off, a group of Hearts fans went round to their end and kicked it off with their boys as they were going into the ground. Just a taster of what they would get afterwards.

The match was a typical Cup tie with Queen Of The South playing out of their skins, and in truth they were the better team. However, a 1-1 draw was a result that we were happy with, leaving us confident for the replay at Tynecastle. The main talking point of the match however wasn't the game, it was the huge riot that erupted in the Hearts end during the second half. This was the first time that I can remember that the problems between Edinburgh and Livingston surfaced at football. Most of the Livi lads were skinheads and they were always mobbed up and, as a result, stood out as a distinct firm amongst the Hearts support. They were very tasty and didn't mess around if they got any grief, which they demonstrated at this match as a full scale battle was fought. When the police waded in to break it up everyone steamed into them as well. The police must have been well fucked off. All the security measures that they had taken to keep rival fans apart in the ground had worked. Instead we'd kicked it off amongst ourselves!

With about ten minutes remaining, the main core of the Hearts firm left the ground along with their opposite numbers from Queen Of The South. The two sides met up on the waste ground outside the ground and a pitched battle was fought. They were well up for it and were doing well, but what turned things in our favour, was the battle was occurring in full view of the away terrace, and reinforcements were soon streaming out the ground to boost our numbers, causing the home mob to back off. The police appeared on horses and managed to separate the sides, but as they charged the Hearts fans and sent some of us jumping into gardens to escape, a few house windows were smashed as well.

By the time the full time whistle went most of the trouble was over and we were able to get onto our buses and start the journey home with few problems. That was the last time that I've been to Dumfries. It was one of my favourite destinations in the hooligan days. They were well game and were one of the few clubs (possibly the only club) that put up any decent resistance while we were in Division One.

We won the replay 1-0 and drew East Fife in the next round at Tynecastle. What should have been an easy match turned out to be quite a close run thing as we squeezed through with a 2-1 win. The only encouraging thing that day was the crowd. 9,300 turning out, proving that a successful team could still draw the crowds. So, through to the Quarter Finals with an away tie at Celtic to look forward to!

The tie certainly caught the imagination and Hearts contributed around six or seven thousand towards the day's attendance of 25,400. It was a total buzz to be visiting both Rangers and Celtic in the same season and we were well game. Right from the start, we gave the lads 100% backing with a wide variety of Hearts chants and party songs coming out of the Hearts end.

As expected though, Celtic took the lead after 12 minutes. However, rather than that breaking us, we stepped up a gear and soon it was all Hearts. We hit the woodwork three times (O'Connor hitting the bar, Johnston and MacDonald hitting the post) and Celtic were barely holding out. The noise from the Hearts end was deafening.

Then two incidents occurred that would change the course of the game and would implant a deep hatred for Celtic amongst many Hearts fans that exists to this day. Firstly, that fine upstanding Scottish international, Danny McGrain, breaks Peter Shields leg with a brutal, typically filthy tackle. Secondly, as we were struggling to come to terms with the fact that McGrain was allowed to remain on the pitch, Davie Provan decided to show the world his acting skills. As he prepared to take a throw-in, Willie Johnston gave him a sarcastic pat on the head. Provan's reaction was to throw himself to the ground as if he had spotted a tenner! It was a cynical attempt by Provan to get a fellow professional sent off and, thanks to the usual pro-Glasgow bias from the referee coupled with Johnston's reputation, it worked. As the referee showed Johnston the red card amidst scenes of chaos, the Hearts bench had to forcefully remove him from the pitch, keeping him away from the officials.

It was also the cue for a full scale riot to erupt in the Hearts end. Due to the segregation, we couldn't get at the Celtic firm so the police did as a substitute and they took a hammering. One after another they disappeared as they were punched to the ground and set upon by the crowd. The loud cheers every time a copper disappeared and his hat was thrown into the air indicated that a large portion of the Hearts support weren't exactly shocked by what was happening.

My only regret is that we didn't invade the pitch. It was all there for us. The Celtic fans were shitting themselves, the police had been battered, and we could have scattered that ground. A lot of Celtic fans have since claimed that if we had got onto the pitch, the Jungle would have killed us. No chance. Hearts wouldn't have ran from anyone that day - basic Edinburgh pride would have made it impossible for us to have run. We had the most useful support in Scotland then and we could have proved it beyond a shadow of a doubt by running Celtic (on TV) inside their own ground. Instead we made do, giving it to them in the streets after the match.

The second half was one way traffic for the home side as they took advantage of the extra man and strolled to a 4-1 victory. Their mouthy fans were giving it large and it was a very dangerous Hearts support that emerged from Parkhead that day. It kicked off almost immediately as we started to walk back to where the buses were parked. As we crossed the main road, a few Celtic fans mistakenly believed that they were safe due to the police presence and started mouthing off at us. They got absolutely leathered as literally hundreds of people waded into them. The police then moved in and got battered for the second time that day as every Celtic fan in the vicinity became a legitimate target. A lot of their fighters had come round to our end after what we had done in the ground and they got slapped silly. It was wild, they were running everywhere and Hearts were punching fuck out of them. So much for all that Glasgow shite about No Mean City and the hardman reputation. They certainly didn't live up to it that day as Edinburgh showed them what it was really all about. Celtic expected us to run when they had a pop and they didn't have a fucking clue what to do when we steamed into them. They were living off a reputation that had disappeared with The Gorbals.

Like most Hearts fans, I have a strong dislike for both Rangers and Celtic, although after that day, I'd side with a Rangers stranger against a Celtic fan any day. This has got nothing to do with any of the religious crap, but is purely based on the fact that Celtic are always trying to give it the disadvantaged underdog, when in reality they are as much a part of the Scottish football establishment as Rangers, and have benefited from numerous dodgy decisions over the years.

Anyway, after all that, Hearts were out of the Cup, and only had the league to concentrate on. In hindsight, the Cup exit was probably a blessing in disguise, enabling the players to be totally focused on promotion, but it was hard to see it that way at the time.

# Chapter Eight

Just after the Celtic match, myself and a few of my mates all got scooters. Despite knowing deep down that the mod scene was on its last legs, it was something that we'd always dreamt about. So it was a fitting way to mark my last few months as a mod. For those of you who know about scooters, it wasn't exactly top of the range, but at the time I was well happy with my Vespa 100 Sport complete with back rest, numerous wing mirrors, crash bars, and an extra spotlight. In fact the only problem with the scooter was the fact that it was green!

There were a few scooter clubs in Edinburgh then, the main one being the Edinburgh Blues (which is still going strong today). Other clubs were the Corrie & District, Edinburgh & District and the East Lothian Scooter Club. Around that time, the scooter scene was beginning to split as people drifted away from the mod thing and became scooter boys. Although the two factions co-exist happily enough now, there was a degree of animosity between the two groups initially. The mods felt that the scooter boys were scruffy with their psychobilly hairdos, Doc Martens, and army greens, riding around on stripped down scooters. On the other hand, the scooter boys saw the mods as snobbish and backward looking. A bit of truth from both sides really, but because I never got involved with any of the scooter clubs, I kept out of that rivalry.

As there were quite a few of us who had scooters who were all mates, we just kicked around together. It was an excellent feeling, around ten of us riding along Princes Street on a Saturday afternoon on the mod customised scooters. A great pose, and it attracted a fair share of female interest too, so most of the day was spent parked up in St Andrew Square trying to impress groups of modettes. Not a bad way to spend a Saturday afternoon, but I missed a few Hearts games playing with my new toy.

As the summer arrived, there were runs out to North Berwick and over to Fife to occupy us, and riding up to mod discos where we would spend most of our time posing outside on the bikes rather than inside. With so many nickable parts, you didn't really want to leave it unguarded. It was a good scene for a while, and it did breathe a little bit of life back into the mod thing. We used to drink down The Royal Mile, in pubs such as The Blue Blanket, Royal

Archer, and a pub called Close Encounters, which was in a close just off the Royal Mile and was to become our main meeting place. The main disco for mods then was the Eclipse Youth Club which had a do every Saturday night at a hall called the Cephas Cellar in Queensferry Street Lane.

The main mob at Cephas Cellar was a mod gang that drank in Elliotts (now The Rutland) which contained one of the main faces on the Edinburgh scene, a bloke who despite being a Hibs fan, was to become one of my best mates. Them along with the remnants of the Gillie Mods and some of the Danderhall Beat Boys.

Another mainstream under 18s disco that was taken over by the mods was Cinderellas on a Tuesday night. This was a great venue and was one of Edinburgh's best nightclubs at the time. It was another club that had a door policy, banning skinheads, and again this resulted in a few incidents when the club chucked out at 11pm, with running battles back to Princes Street. Unfortunately, we seemed to be doing most of the running. The skinhead scene was on its last legs as well though, and the trouble was nowhere as serious or frequent as it would've been six months ago.

As well as the clubs, a new band had been formed by former 9 Below Zero frontman, Dennis Greaves. Called The Truth, they were to all intents and purposes a mod band, and they had a pop / Jam sound. The band went onto have a few hits and some *Top Of The Pops* appearances, but the highlight of that spring was their gig at The Nite Club a few weeks before their *Top Of The Pops* debut. A great night at a good venue which seemed packed with a crowd of around 250-300, most of whom were mods. Superb atmosphere, and great when you knew about 90% of the crowd.

\* \* \*

Anyway, back to the football. After the Cup exit, it was all go for promotion, and we bounced back with a 4-0 home win in front of 7,000 against Partick Thistle. The results were going our way and the next big game for the lads was away at Airdrie on Saturday, the 2nd of April. Airdrie was a horrible little town, full of headcases (still is), and despite the fact that many of their lads would've supported the Glasgow teams, they were more than willing to fight for their home town team too. Their ground, Broomfield Park, was a bit of a dump, although it did have the obligatory covered terracing segregated along the half way line which is so common in Scotland.

50

All of their boys stood right up against the fence and spent most the game staring us out and throwing coins rather than watching the game. Calling themselves the Section B, they made repeated surges towards the fence chanting, "1, 2, 3, who are we? We are the mental Section B!", as they threw their missiles and gobbed at us. As per normal, the Old Bill did nothing about them, but steamed into us when we had a go at the fence. Cue the almost compulsory ruck with the coppers and about five minutes of fists flying, crowd surges and police hats being thrown into the air, before it all calmed down. Hearts ran out 2-0 winners so the locals weren't best amused as the game came to an end. As we came out the ground, the Section B charged us, throwing bricks, bottles and other missiles. Hearts charged back and it was toe to toe for a while until the police separated the fans. It went off again around our buses too as the Airdrie mob smashed a few bus windows before being chased off. A very enjoyable Saturday which was rounded off by pulling a bird in Close Encounters that night.

As the end of the season approached, Hearts went into their traditional bad run of results. A 2-1 defeat at St Johnstone was followed by a 2-2 draw at home to Clydebank, 1-1 away at Alloa, and 3-3 at home to Dunfermline (after being 3-1 up). The last three games should have given us maximum points, but it looked as if the typical lack of bottle for the big occasions was affecting the team again. A re-run of the previous season was on the cards with Clydebank and Partick Thistle closing the gap to only two points. We only needed two points from our last two games, but the next match was away at bogey team Dumbarton, and with the previous season's 5-2 defeat still fresh in the mind, we weren't exactly looking forward to it. Our final game was at home to Hamilton Accies.

So, on Saturday, the 7th of May, me and my mates along with around 3,000 other Hearts fans (the crowd was 4,000) went on the club buses to Boghead. The atmosphere on the buses was tense to say the least on the way through. Boghead had never been a happy hunting ground for Hearts and everyone realised that failure to get promotion this season would all but finish the club off. Once in the ground however, we outnumbered the home fans three to one and we soon got behind the team right from the kick-off. The Dumbarton fans kept quiet - a full scale riot by Hearts fans during a visit to Boghead in the Seventies was no doubt still fresh in a good few memories.

This time the game went in our favour. The experienced heads of Willie Johnston, Sandy Jardine, Alex MacDonald, and Derek O'Connor ensured the young playmakers of the Hearts team kept their nerve. We began to relax after John Robertson put us 1-0 up in 13 minutes, and four minutes later when he made it two, we were wondering what all the worrying was about. Derek O'Connor and Gary McKay added two more to see Hearts come out comfortable 4-0 winners.

As the full time whistle went, hundreds of us charged past the police onto the pitch. The players took our acclaim by reappearing in the directors box of the main stand. It was mental, here we were on the pitch at Boghead celebrating promotion to the Premier League and we were going mad like we had won the European Cup or something. It was basically relief. We knew how close we had come to oblivion and we knew what a gamble it was for Wallace Mercer to decide to stay a full time club at the end of the previous season.

As St Johnstone had drawn that day we were now only one point behind them, with a goal difference of around 20 better than them and one game to go. We were at home to Hamilton and if we won and St Johnstone dropped a point to Dunfermline we would be champions. The excitement of the day and the fact that Hearts reduced their prices as a thanks to the fans resulted in a 9,000 crowd inside Tynecastle (with only about 50 of them being Hamilton fans) to see us cruise to a 2-0 win.

Unfortunately, when the result came over from Muirton Park, it told us that St Johnstone were champions by one point courtesy of a 1-0 win.. A bit of a disappointment, but the promotion was the main thing and the fans were in full voice as the celebrations started in earnest. How different an atmosphere it was from 12 months previously. This time Wallace Mercer took part in the team's lap of honour as opposed to dodging coins as he tried to stop a riot last May. The hatred had been replaced by the optimism of Ibrox, Parkhead, Easter Road, Pittodrie. The Hearts were back!

# Chapter Nine

The day after the Hamilton match, it was a case of getting over the hangovers quickly for a visit to Easter Road for the Jim McArthur (Hibs' goalie) testimonial between us and Hibs. It was a fairly lacklustre match, which Hibs won 4-2. However, we managed one more ruck to mark the end of the season. During the match it kicked off with the police in the Dunbar End and there was also a bit of scrapping on the East Terrace as some Hearts fans infiltrated the home end. After the scenes following the Tom Hart Memorial, it was a wonder that Hibs invited us to play another "friendly" anyway!

The rest of the summer was spent being a mod. On Friday, the 17th of June, we all met up in Princes Street on scooters with the Edinburgh Blues and Corrie & District scooter clubs and rode out to Dunbar for the National Scooter Run. As we rode through Edinburgh we all kept in formation, about 40 to 50 scooters, which certainly stopped people in their tracks as we went past. The whole weekend was a good laugh with a crowd of around 3,000 there from all over Britain. However, there were a few too many scooter boys and skinheads there for my liking. A group of East Lothian mods had formed the In Style All Mod Scooter Club which was based in Tranent so we hung around with them most of the time. Although there was a bit of trouble during the weekend, it was nothing serious and we didn't get involved in it. However, the locals gave us a mixed reception with some letting us sleep in their gardens and others being a tad unfriendly towards us.

After Dunbar it was back to job interviews, careers officers, and eventually starting my first job at the beginning of August. Before that we spent most of our days hanging around St James's Centre and going for Cappacinos in the Top Man Cafe. There were quite a few of the mods who had just left school or were unemployed so there was often a decent sized mob of us hanging around. When there was decent weather we'd play putting in Princes Street Gardens in the morning then tour around the shops in the afternoon. Also, as with the previous summer, we'd go through to Glasgow and meet up with some of their mods, and one Saturday we all went down to Newcastle for the day. This ended up in an evening of trouble with the local skinheads before getting the last train back to

Edinburgh. We done fairly well against the Geordies, didn't disgrace ourselves.

Clothes-wise that summer, it was a definite case of dressing down. The suits and jackets were cast aside completely and, as with the previous summer, paisley shirts and cycling tops were all the rage. A white cotton roll neck worn outside a pair of jeans or sta-prest trousers was also a popular look. As far as zip up jackets were concerned, the Fred Perry jackets were THE essential replacing the Harrington. For rainy days, white macs (as per Paul Weller in the *Speak Like A Child* video) were popular.

Anyway, what with starting work and knocking around with the mods, I gave all the pre-season matches a miss this year. But I was raring to go on the 20th of August 20th for the first match back in the Premier League. Away to St Johnstone.

# Chapter Ten

Although not the best opening game that we could've hoped for, a match away at St Johnstone was always good for a laugh. Especially when they played at their original ground, Muirton Park, on the edge of the city centre, which was a real football stadium unlike the shitty soulless retail park that they play at now.

As it was the first game of the season, and seeing as we were back in the top division as well, the turnout from Hearts was very good, with around 3,000 making the short trip to Perth. Their support was a bit disappointing and the actual gate that day was only 6,600. About a dozen or so of us mods went up together on the same train that the main organised firm of Hearts fans, The Service Crew & Saville Travel, went up on. This was pre-casuals, and this mob had been travelling as a firm since the Seventies, so all the claims from Aberdeen that they were the first organised mob in Scotland is wrong. They were the first firm to adopt the casual style, but I know that Hearts, Hibs and Dundee had organised hooligan mobs who travelled by train in the Seventies, and I would imagine that Rangers and Celtic would've as well.

When we got to Perth, the Service Crew hit the pubs and we heard later in the ground that they had a massive punch-up in one of them. We had a stroll around Perth, getting a bite to eat, and eventually finding a boozer that would serve us. We were all quite casually dressed with Fred Perry jackets, cardigans or Harringtons, button down shirts, sta-prest and bowling shoes. We were obviously mods and as we approached the ground around 2.15pm we bumped into the Perth Pack. As previously mentioned, they were mostly skinheads, and when they saw us, all mods with Hearts scarves, it must've been like Christmas come early for them. Although they were a tasty mob and were about 30 handed, we weren't about to run on the first day of the season. As there were loads of Hearts fans around, we charged them, giving it the large one with all the outstretched arms. As they started to come towards us the other Hearts fans jumped in too (just as we had hoped), and the St Johnstone mob backed off, chucking a couple of bottles, just as the police came and put us in the ground.

As 3pm approached, the excitement of being back in the Premier League was evident as the Hearts support was giving it full volume right from the start, with scuffles breaking out with the police under the covered terracing. We were determined to prove ourselves in the Premier League on and off the pitch. Hearts had made a couple of free transfer signings in the close season, bringing in George Cowie, a 22 year old from West Ham, and the experienced veteran, Jimmy Bone. In what was a very close fought and physical match, Bone scored the only goal of the match midway through the second half to give us a 1 -0 win. We went absolutely mad when that goal went in. Maybe the days of being a yo-yo club were over. It was important for both teams to get that psychological first victory, and with the odds against us, we had done it.

After the match there were a few scuffles outside the ground, but we got away sharpish and made our way quickly back to the station. We knew we had rode our luck with the Perth Pack before the game and we didn't want to invite revenge.

The next two games were against Cowdenbeath in the League Cup, and we had the scenario that all Hearts fans are familiar with. A poor team bringing us down to their level. A dire 0-0 match at arguably the worst ground in senior football, Central Park, on the Wednesday. This was followed by an equally bad match at Tynecastle on the Saturday, where after a 1-1 scoreline, Hearts scraped through 4-2 on penalties. Just as well the away goal rule didn't apply then. The only good thing to come from those two mind numbingly boring matches was the fact that we would sign their star player, Craig Levein, later in the season, who, as you all know, would go on to become a Tynecastle favourite. Anyway, the penalty victory meant that we qualified for the League Cup Sections, where we were drawn in a group against Rangers, St Mirren and Clydebank.

The following Wednesday, we got a 2-2 draw at Love Street, with Jimmy Bone scoring again and John Robertson netting a penalty for us. Further proof that we would be able to hold our own in the Premier League this time around.

Saturday, the 3rd of September, saw the first of the four Edinburgh derby matches this season. After our fairly decent start, a crowd of over 20,000 turned up to see Hearts defeat our rivals at last. Hibs took the lead in the first half and their goal was greeted with the obligatory "You're gonna get your fuckin' heads kicked in!" chant. This was followed by an outbreak of fighting in the corner of the Shed. At that time (hard as it is to believe now), Hibs always used to beat us and it looked as if things were going the same way again. But the second half was to serve up a cracker of a match. Shortly after the restart, Robbo scored a spectacular equaliser sending us wild. But Irvine then put Hibs back in front. Again Robertson popped up to equalise for us and most of the Hearts fans would've settled for a 2-2 draw. But with only 14 minutes left, that man Jimmy Bone headed a winner.

The scenes in the home end were ecstatic and as a result it was a largely good natured Hearts support that left the ground. Therefore, there was a minimal amount of trouble on Gorgie Road. In the city centre it was a different story however, as a group of Hibs fans attacked Hearts fans in St James's Centre and smashed a few shop windows into the bargain.

The games were coming thick and fast and the following Wednesday saw the first of a double header against Rangers at Tynecastle. This match was a League Cup match and a disappointing crowd of only 11,000 saw Hearts well beaten 3-0. On the Saturday, however, we got our revenge and won 3-1 in the league in front of over 16,000. After this match, I took my first bad kicking at football when Rangers done Hearts on Gorgie Road afterwards. As usual, there were a few punches thrown outside the Tynecastle Arms pub where the two groups of fans met up. It looked as if Hearts were going to do the business again, with all of us walking in the middle of the road giving them the come ahead. However, as we went under the old railway bridge, the Rangers fans charged us from the front and side and Hearts were soon running back up Gorgie Road. I took a punch to the back of the head, stumbled, and was set upon straight away. I curled into a ball as the kicks rained in and I was only saved when Hearts charged back and Rangers backed off. A few older Hearts fans helped me up and managed to drag me into the Tynecastle Arms before Rangers once again sent the Hearts fans scattering back along the road.

I was well out of it. I couldn't stand up without any help and my head was spinning. However, the staff in the pub were great and after about half an hour, I managed to get myself together enough to get a bus home with only a couple of bruises to remind me of the kicking. If the fans who dragged me into the pub are reading this, cheers for helping me out.

That was the first time that I had really seen Hearts get done at home. Apparently, there were running battles that day all the way back to Haymarket Station with the Rangers lads doing the business the vast majority of the time. Welcome to the Premier League!

The following couple of weeks were good for me. I started seeing this mod bird and it was full on sex right from the start. But this was topped by Hearts winning run in the league continuing with two great away wins at Dundee (2-1) and at St Mirren (1-0). I was at both those matches and I can't recall anything going on at Dens Park, but it did kick off again at Love Street. Again, it was with the police at the segregation fence in the covered terracing along the side of the pitch. About three quarters of Hearts 2,000 travelling support were crowded into this section and it was a fairly major incident with fans at the front of the terracing having to jump over onto the running track to escape crushing. After the game we also charged the home supporters and chased them up the road on our way back to the buses.

\* \* \*

All good things have to come to an end however. Firstly, I crashed my scooter and ended up in hospital overnight. Nothing too serious, just a bit of concussion and a few minor cuts, but the bike was a write off and all there was to look forward to was the insurance money. With the accident, I decide that it was time for a change, and when the insurance money came through it would be spent on a new wardrobe. I didn't know what exactly yet, but I would find out the following Saturday!

I went to the Hearts - Aberdeen match with my dad. He had stopped going in the mid Seventies, finding watching a declining club with an increasing hooligan problem a bit too painful. He had started to show a bit of an interest again with our impressive start and I had persuaded him to come along. I suppose that was always going to be a bad move. It started off well enough however, getting to the ground around 2pm and getting a seat in the main stand to watch the ground start to fill up with an impressive attendance (it was over 18,000) and see the team get a great welcome from the fans. However, it wasn't long before Aberdeen were showing us why they would end up winning the league that season and in all honestly they cruised to a 2-0 victory.

As me and my dad left the ground, we got to the top of McLeod Street just as the Hearts mob were wading into a group of around 100 lads with no club colours on. Those guys looked well cool. All wedge haircuts, Pringle sweaters, bleached or stonewashed Lois jeans and white trainers. Although they were

58

taking a bit of a hiding and were backing off, they didn't run and they kept having a go back. I'll always remember them chanting, 'Aber-deen Soccer Casuals!' as they kept coming back at the Hearts.

I was fascinated by it all, but my main concern was to get my dad out safely as the mounted police were sending people scattering in all directions. We managed to fight our way out the crush and back to the car. Needless to say, my dad wasn't as impressed with his introduction to the casual movement as I was. In fact, he never set foot back inside a football ground again.

I was really impressed with the look of the casuals at that match. One of my mates had been dressing in that style since the spring but I hadn't really paid much attention to it. However, after that introduction I was interested in finding out more. *Sounds* music newspaper and *The Face* magazine were the best reference points, with the letters pages of Sounds full of letters from casuals, scallies and perries as London, Liverpool and Manchester fought a war of words as to who was first to adopt the designer look on the terraces. Then there were the letters from gangs such as the Derby Lunatic Fringe, the Pompey 6:57 Crew, the Chelsea Headhunters, and the Millwall Bushwackers amongst others, to introduce me to a whole new world. Letters from the Aberdeen (ASC) mob also featured quite prominently, and it actually angered me that they were in on this and we didn't have a clue about what was going on. There were even specialist shops catering for the movement, and from what I could make out from the letters, Stewarts in Shepherds Bush, West London, and Street Fighter in Birmingham were the two main outlets. I couldn't wait for the insurance money to come through.

But what really done it for me was when there was a reference to the Motherwell Saturday Service, "the best dressed in the west". Motherwell had a casual mob as well. It was hard to understand why this new fashion from England had caught on in Aberdeen and Motherwell, but didn't appear to have made any impact on Edinburgh or Glasgow.

However, on the Tuesday after the Aberdeen match it was another night out with the mods. The Truth were playing at the Edinburgh University Students Union in Bistro Square, so a few of us went along to see them. There was a much reduced mod presence outside the venue as the cult was dropping in numbers all the time by now. Maybe down to only 70 or 80 by this time.

Anyway, it was obviously still enough to worry the management of the venue as they were insisting on applying a students only ruling. At first we were trying to get students to sign us in as their guests, but those snotty wankers didn't want to know. It was infuriating. We had been into the band right from the start, but now they'd had a hit single, all these bandwagon jumpers were getting in and we weren't. Well, you aren't going to take that are you? At first we caused a bit of a fuss at the door and demanded to see the band. Dennis Greaves, being a good bloke, came out to speak to us. Apparently the venue had assured the band that all their fans would get in and had just changed the door policy at the last minute. The band were having words with them, but there was nothing really that they could do. So after that the only option was to try to break in.

We went around the side of the hall and found a fire exit which we promptly kicked in. Luckily, quite a few got in that way before the security came down and chased us off. The adrenalin was pumping now and those that hadn't got in steamed around the front and up to the main entrance. The main face of the Elliotts pub mod gang smacked the bloke taking the tickets and we all charged in. They just stood back and let us get on with it, and by the time the bouncers had got themselves sorted out, we were in the main hall mingling in with crowd so they just left it. It was a worthwhile effort as The Truth played an excellent set and Dennis Greaves dedicated a song "to all the mods down the front".

The next few games were drawn, including 1-1 away at Celtic. A game, incidentally that was attended by only 12,207, of which around 3,000 were Hearts fans. An attendance like that makes a mockery of the "loyal supporters" tag that the media gives the Old Firm's fans. Rangers weren't any better as I have already mentioned, their fans obviously not being able to handle a couple of seasons without winning any silverware. Maybe they should try going 36 years without winning anything. If that happened, I think Rangers and Celtic would go bust. The next time any Old Firm fan tries to slag you about the size of our support, just point out to them that they are glory hunters and remind them how low their support had fallen to in the early Eighties.

Despite the draws, the team was still doing well and was keeping a healthy cushion between ourselves and the relegation zone. The good start, together with the experience of the older heads, had helped our younger players gain a bit of confidence, and this was showing in our results. All too often, a promoted team gets so many defeats as they are adjusting to the Premier League, that by the time they have adjusted, they have had all their confidence beaten out of them, and before you know it, they're adrift in the relegation positions.

# Chapter Eleven

The insurance money came through towards the end of October, and I'd soon have a new image. A quick shopping trip and I was kitted out in a Pringle, Sergio Tachinni tennis shirt, Lois Jeans, Nike Wimbledons, and a Nike rain jacket. The hair was also growing into an above the ears wedge, and would shortly be stepped at the back. The Hearts scarf was cast aside, an act which I know many readers would not have approved of. That seemed to be part of the opposition from the main body of Hearts supporters towards casuals. They felt that it was cowardly not to wear colours, whereas the casuals would argue that by not wearing scarves, they could infiltrate amongst the opposition fans with greater ease, and therefore cause more trouble. I just stopped wearing a scarf because a cheap football scarf didn't really go with clothes that you had spent hundreds of pounds on.

Guy Fawkes night saw us visit Easter Road for the second derby of the season, and again there was a substantial amount of trouble at this game. Before the match, Hearts and Hibs fans clashed in St James's Centre, which resulted in a running battle on the pedestrian bridge over Leith Street, which continued down the grass slope on the other side of the road. There were further incidents outside the Playhouse. However the main ruck before the match erupted at the top of Easter Road. The main group of Hearts fans coming along London Road arrived at the top of Easter Road at the same time as a group of Hibs fans who were coming along from Meadowbank. The Hibs fans fronted up the Hearts contingent who charged at them, which resulted in running battles right down Easter Road. It was mayhem as the Hibs fans kept steaming back, despite being gradually forced down the road. The police eventually managed to charge the Hearts fans off the main road into the side street and over the foot bridge towards the away end. At first, the police were met by a hail of stones and bottles, but eventually they managed to disperse the Hearts fans.

Inside the ground, the atmosphere was pretty heavy and the consequence of playing an Edinburgh derby on Guy Fawkes night was the stream of fireworks that were flying between the two groups of fans over the segregation fence. The match itself was a typically hard fought derby and we were pleased with a 1-1 draw courtesy of a John Robertson goal. Robbo, of course, would become a thorn in the side of Hibs with an excellent goalscoring record against them.

After the game, there was a bit of nonsense in London Road, with some Hearts fans smashing cars that were stuck in the gridlocked traffic, and when the police first arrived on the scene, they too were attacked, but they soon had things under control.

The next few games, gave a mixed bag of results with a few fairly heavy defeats, the worst being going down 3-0 at Ibrox and 3-1 at home to Celtic. The Celtic match was another lively day in Gorgie with some trouble in the ground (mainly missiles onto the pitch), and running battles in Gorgie Road after the match which seemed to go on for ages before the police sorted things out.

As Christmas approached, although our form had dipped a bit in recent weeks, we were still not too badly placed in the league and were looking good bets to avoid relegation. The traditional New Year fixture, which was played on the 2nd of January at Tynecastle, attracted our biggest home gate of the season, 23,500, who witnessed a fairly entertaining 1-1 draw. Although it was quite a subdued derby, Hearts fans attacked Hibs supporters as they made their way back along the Gorgie Road after the match.

Bad weather forced the cancellation of many games in the next few weeks and my next match was our Scottish Cup Third Round tie against Partick Thistle at Tynecastle which we won 2-0 on a Monday night in February. The following Saturday we got a good 2-2 draw at home against Rangers with Hearts rediscovering their early season form.

Due to the amount of matches that had been postponed, I'd been knocking around town on a Saturday afternoon a lot with the mods again. Although I was going up dressed casual at the time, there was no problem, as unlike other cities (particularly in England), there was no rivalry in Edinburgh between the two groups. Of course, at that time hardly anyone in Edinburgh new anything about casuals. Apart from me and my mate, I certainly never knew any other casuals personally, although there were a small group around who called themselves the Capital City Casuals. The only reason that I knew of their existence was a bit of graffiti at St Andrew Square Bus Station that would remain there for years. From what I've found out since, the Capital City Casuals numbered six or seven (at most), and although they weren't really a football mob, they were Hibs supporters.

On the mod scene, although the numbers were drastically reduced from the heyday, there was still quite an active scene in Edinburgh. Most of it centred around an Edinburgh band called The Pride, who, although not mods themselves, looked the part and definitely sounded the business with a sound that was heavily influenced by The Jam. They wrote all their own stuff and played various gigs around Edinburgh, and were always brilliant live. As well as The Pride, there was a band called The Mirrors from West Lothian. They were an out and out mod / Sixties band and had a more poppy feel compared to the aggressive sound of The Pride. Although they were good, The Mirrors played too many cover versions for me, and as such I always preferred The Pride.

Although the amount of mods in Edinburgh city centre had decreased, there were fairly good scenes coming through in the towns around Edinburgh. West Lothian had an up and coming scene with a fairly sizeable mob who used to follow The Mirrors everywhere. Centred on the small town of East Calder, they were to promote some great mod nights in the near future. On the other side of Edinburgh, based in the East Lothian town of Tranent, was the previously mentioned In Style All Mod Scooter Club. These groups would usually come into Edinburgh on a Saturday afternoon so there were quite a lot of mods and scooters floating about, and things were beginning to kick off again. On the 4th of February, a huge mod gang, well in excess of 100, staged running battles with the police, firstly in Cockburn Street and then around St James's Centre. One of the Edinburgh faces was nicked and as the police were trying to get him into the van, loads of people steamed into them. We were unsuccessful in getting him released, and the arrival of a few dog handlers soon managed to disperse the mob.

The next round of the Scottish Cup saw us drawn away to Dundee United on Saturday, the 18th of February. A good travelling support of around 4,000 went up. This was a bit of a niggle match due to the bad blood between the two clubs over unpaid transfer fees by Hearts two seasons previously. A crowd of just under 14,500 provided a pretty heavy atmosphere throughout the game. We were in the covered terracing along the side of the pitch, which was segregated at the halfway line. Throughout the first half they were chucking missiles at us as we surged towards the fence. As usual, the police were only nicking visiting fans for retaliating, and the mood began to turn ugly amongst the Hearts support.

The ill feeling between the clubs was also evident on the pitch and there were quite a few incidents between the players. Three minutes before the interval, a clash between Jimmy Bone and Paul Hegarty of Dundee United resulted in Bone being sent off. This was too much for the Hearts support and the away terrace erupted with trouble. There were repeated attempts to break down the segregation fence, and when the police moved in everyone turned on them.

As the players left the pitch for half-time, there was a full scale battle raging on the terracing between us and the Old Bill, causing fans to spill over onto the pitch. Fighting also broke out on the running track as police were attacked while leading an arrested Hearts fan around the pitch. The police managed to calm the crowd during the interval, but further trouble erupted towards the end of the match when United scored the winner (2-1 the final score) from what looked like an offside position.

As we left the ground it was obvious that there would be further trouble. Any United fan that we came across on the way back to the buses was beaten, and a street battle erupted when a group of United fans started to taunt us. Once again, the Hearts support turned their attention to the police due to the lack of serious opposition from the home fans, and for a while we had the upper hand before more police arrived in numbers. Another job well done.

Now out of the Cup, it just left league survival to concentrate on, and with wins over Motherwell and St Mirren in March, we ensured that Premier League football would be played at Tynecastle the following season.

The last derby match of the season was at Easter Road where 19,000 watched a dour 0-0 draw. Again there was trouble before and after the match around Easter Road and London Road. After Hibs, the next biggie was home to Aberdeen on Wednesday, the 2nd of May. Aberdeen turned up with a huge support and a huge mob, as a win would see them lift the championship. There was little trouble before the match, but after Aberdeen won 1-0, serious violence erupted in the streets. Hundreds of Hearts fans went round to the away end to wait for the celebrating Aberdeen fans to come out. When they did, the casuals were at the front of their support and it went off big style. Twice Aberdeen were chased back into the ground before the police could disperse the Hearts fans. Further trouble also broke out all the way back to Haymarket station in one of the most violent nights that I have ever witnessed at football.

Although Aberdeen were undoubtedly a top firm, they got a hiding that night. Sheer weight of numbers had them running in all directions, as Hearts lost it big time. There were people being pulled from buses and hammered, casuals going through windows. Totally mental.

We then played Celtic on the 5th of May, where a 1-1 draw meant that not only had we avoided relegation, but we had qualified for the last UEFA Cup place and had finished above Hibs. Not bad for our first season back in the big time. After the Celtic match, there were two more games which I missed due to dating a girl that I would end up seeing every day over the summer. A record for me at the time.

Casuals were by now notorious throughout Scotland following a full scale battle inside Fir Park back in February between the visiting Aberdeen Soccer Casuals and the Motherwell Saturday Service. The game was held up as the two mobs fought a pitched battle, putting the casual cult firmly on the map. The police didn't have a clue as Aberdeen infiltrated the home end thanks to the lack of football colours being worn, and when the fighting started, they still didn't have a clue because both mobs were casual. They also found it hard to control the numbers that were involved, with Aberdeen's mob being around 600 strong and Motherwell having around 300 tops.

The trouble continued outside after the match with running battles breaking out everywhere. The Motherwell police certainly learned the hard way about the threat that the casuals posed, particularly since the violence was organised to an extent never really witnessed in Scotland before. This trouble had been brewing for a while, and prior to the battle it had been fought through the letters pages of *Sounds*. The dispute centred around who was the original Casual mob in Scotland, and also who were the hardest. Now, although I'm not 100% sure, I'd say that Aberdeen just shaded it in both departments, although fair play to the Saturday Service because they weren't long behind Aberdeen. What I will say about Motherwell is that their mob had the best name in the Scottish casual scene, with their baby crew also having a good name in the Tufty Club.

Anyway, after this battle, the media went to town, doing their bit to save the nation from this evil new cult. The *Daily Record* sent a reporter to Aberdeen's next away match against Kilmarnock to interview a few of the casuals, and to give a breakdown of what clothes they were wearing. This article appeared in the paper on the Friday, and gave me a bit of explaining to do as my mum now knew the score about the casuals.

That summer though, the casual fashions changed. Pringles were out, and were replaced by Fila ski jumpers, jeans were worn with a split in the ankle and were left frayed at the bottom, and Diadora trainers were compulsory, with the Borg Elite style also being casual must haves, the gold flash making them stand out from the crowd. Jumbo cords were also worn around this time and at the start of the new season.

Hearts had a little mob by now who were dressing casual and who were calling themselves the Casual Soccer Firm (CSF). They had first appeared near the end of the season at Dundee United away in the league, and had got legged off the small mob of Dundee United casuals who called themselves the Tayside Trendies at the time, but then again we only had about five lads and they had about 30. Over on the other side of Edinburgh, Hibs were also beginning to pull in the numbers and were getting a good firm together under the name of the Capital City Service (CCS).

In town during the summer you would see other casuals on occasion, especially in Austin Reed on Princes Street. Their sports department was the only place in Edinburgh that stocked Fila sportswear, and was a must place to shop for any up and coming casual. Being so few in numbers, there were no problems between Hearts and Hibs at the time, and everyone used to talk to each other. I didn't really knock about with the other Hearts lads then anyway, and was either with my old mod mates or usually with my girlfriend.

The mod scene was having a bit of a second wind in the summer of '84. At the Maybury Hotel in May, around 200 mods (and me) attended a great night, with The Pride and The Mirrors both playing storming sets. London band, Small World, were meant to be playing too, but they pulled out at the last minute, but it was still a great night nevertheless.

Although that was a memorable night, the summer of '84 has to be best remembered as the summer of northern soul in Edinburgh, with everyone tuning into the best music out. The Jack Kane Centre in Niddrie put on a few excellent allnighters and that was definitely the place to be seen. I remember going to my first niter and being totally bowled over by it. There were a few of us from our estate that used to go and it was blinding. Soul boys, scooter boys, mods, skinheads, casuals, all speeding out their heads, totally on it, having a night out with no problems. Everyone was doing whizz in pill form rather than just powder - that came later. The main pills were Black & Whites, Dexys, and Bombers for the hardened night owl. The sounds were brilliant, with some of the top DJs on the soul scene playing. The usual two room format, the main room was all '60s, and the small room and chill out area was for modern soul.

It was good to see a few early casuals attending the niters. After all, northern soul has to be the definitive music for the Saturday Boys, and in the early to mid Eighties, most of the niters in England would be attended by a fair few football firms. Respect goes out to the BBC from Sheffield, the Hull mob, the Baby Squad at Leicester, and the Guvnors at Manchester City with regard to this. Up north too there was a fairly active soul scene in Aberdeen and a fair amount of their boys would be in attendance, and the same was true with Motherwell who used to make the Shotts niters their second home.

So, that was the summer of '84. Mod nights, northern soul alinighters, loads of speed, and my first fairly serious relationship. For once, I never thought too much about the forthcoming season, although that all changed once it started because the following two seasons were to become the years of the casual!

# Chapter Twelve

Being as loved up as I was meant that I missed all the friendlies which consisted of a pre-season tour to the Highlands. I also missed our first two league matches of the season away at Dundee United where we went down 2-0, a home defeat by Morton 2-1, and the 4-0 League Cup victory over East Stirling at Tynecastle. However, I was at the first Edinburgh derby of the season at Easter Road. A match that even Hearts assistant boss, Sandy Jardine, described as scandalous!

There wasn't enough casuals on either side for there to be any trouble between the respective mobs, but there was a riot in the Hearts end during the match in what was the scarfers' last big day. Once again, the trouble erupted due to tension between Edinburgh and Livingston. As a full scale battle raged amongst the Hearts fans in the Dunbar End, the players on the pitch seemed to be copying us as they produced one of the ugliest Edinburgh derby matches, with constant fouling and off the ball incidents.

The police came into the terracing in force and managed to contain the situation. However, further trouble erupted just after Paul Kane put Hibs in front shortly before half-time. Some Hearts fans ran onto the pitch and fighting broke out once again in the Dunbar End. Also during the first half, there was a constant barrage of missiles thrown at the Hibs goalie, Alan Rough, who was struck on the head by a large marble during the warm up. Lumps of concrete, golf balls, bottles, and coins littered the goalmouth, and the ones that fell short injured numerous Hearts fans who were standing at the front of the terracing. It was some of the most serious terracing trouble that I have ever witnessed inside a football ground.

Just after half-time, a Craig Levein equaliser improved the mood amongst the Hearts support and as the fans were making their way towards the exits, a Derek O'Connor strike gave Hearts the winner in the dying seconds of the match. Which sent the away support delirious. As people swayed down towards the front, more fans spilled onto the pitch again.

There were further confrontations with the police going along London Road after the match, but with the fans in a good mood with the victory, this was pretty tame stuff. However, the damage had already been done with the trouble in the ground, with the referee sure to mention it in his report and the media equally certain to pick up on it. With us having drawn Paris St Germain in the UEFA Cup, there was much concern about trouble breaking out the following month in Paris. And that prospect was one of the main reasons that I was going.

* * *

As the autumn came in, it was time to get the jackets bought for the winter. In the autumn of '84 in Edinburgh, Fila was THE label for the sussed football fan. This was when Fila produced good quality expensive clothing, not the shite that they do now. Fila Windcheaters, Fila BJs, and Fila ski jackets were the items of clothing to be seen in. I had the windcheater and the ski jacket, but unfortunately, never the Fila BJ, which must go down as an all time classic item of casual clothing. Kagouls were still big and the label to have was Kappa. Again, this was before the label descended into the crap that it is today. The Kappa jacket was well cool at that time and only seemed to be available from Olympus Sport in Glasgow. When I went through to get mine, two Rangers boys showed me where Olympus was, and we had a walk around a few shops in Glasgow. No problems in those days.

It breaks my heart to see how a once great label has now descended to being the essential item of clothing for 13 year old Kappa Slappers on street corners all over Britain. Ever since Damon Albarn of Blur desecrated the label by being pictured wearing the kagoul, it has been downhill all the way.

Pringles had almost gone completely by now, although you could still get away with Lyle & Scott V necks with a Tachinni roll-neck underneath. Likewise, Adidas, Patrick and Nike rain jackets were all out. And with footwear being between ,Diadora Borg Elite or Diadora suede trainers, it was definitely a case of Italian or nothing. Full tracksuits by Tachinni, Fila, or Ellesse were often worn as well. This was something that I never got into as I couldn't see the merits of wearing tracksuit bottoms, but I did jump about in a smart dark blue Tachinni tracksuit top for a bit.

Between the Hibs match and Paris, I didn't get to any other matches as I was saving hard. Hearts in Europe was something that I definitely wouldn't miss. My only taste of European football prior to this was in 1976 when we played Locomotive Leipzig and SV Hamburg. Obviously I only got to the home games with my dad, but the bug had definitely bitten. The 5-1 win over Leipzig at Tynecastle in front of 18,000 is still one of my all time best football memories. A very average Hearts side were simply superb that night as Bobby Prentice tore the Germans apart on the wing. Unfortunately, the result in the next round was not so memorable.

Anyway, the trip to Paris had been booked and it had skinted me. Four of us were travelling by train to Dover then over on the ferry and onwards to Paris. We left Edinburgh on Monday, the 17th of September for the game on the Wednesday, and got back on the Friday. It was the first time I'd been abroad with my mates and it was fucking mental.

We had stayed the Monday night in a dodgy B&B just around the corner from London Victoria and had spent the evening drinking around that area. Anyone who knows London will realise that it's not exactly one of the nicer areas, and from what I can remember, the locals were not too amused to have four pissed up Jocks staggering around the pubs! However, we got away with it without any casualties.

Tuesday was a day I'd rather forget as a mixture of hangover and seasickness ensured that the contents of my stomach were deposited into the English Channel on more than one occasion. This kept the large group of Hearts fans on the boat amused for most of the trip! Once in Paris, we booked into a hotel just along from the Gare Du Nord for a couple of nights, and then made our way by the Metro (which was a nightmare) down to the Eiffel Tower where the Hearts fans were meeting up. After getting lost a couple of times and bumping into similar lost souls, we eventually got there. And what a sight! It was like Trafalgar Square on a Wembley weekend . . . pissed up Scots everywhere, jumping about, lying in the gutters, a huge Hearts party in full flow in the centre of Paris!

Most of the fans stayed around that area drinking carry-outs as the bar prices in Paris were a total rip off. As it got late, there were a few scuffles with some PSG fans and also some Africans. Hearts done them fairly easily, the only dodgy bit being when one of the Africans pulled a blade that looked more like a sword and fronted about 30 Hearts fans on his own. Everyone took a couple of steps back, as nobody fancied going in first to get their head sliced open. A few seconds passed with no-one quite knowing what to do, until a Hearts boy ran up behind the African and put a bottle over his head. The bloke went down and got hammered, eventually only being saved by a police charge.

As we made our way back to our B&B on the Metro we had another run-in with the Africans. A Hearts fan had a bum bag strapped around him and a couple of blacks grabbed it as they got off at one of the stations. We steamed off the train, but soon jumped back on when they pulled knives out on us. There was only about £30 worth of francs in it anyway and none of us felt that was worth being cut up for. We had learned the hard way that Paris was a very dangerous city.

The following day, it was the same routine. Down to the Eiffel Tower with a carry-out. There were thousands of fans here by now, with numerous supporters clubs arriving that morning. All in all, there were around 4,000 Hearts fans in the 22,000 crowd at the Parc Des Princes, and despite the 4-0 defeat, we sang our hearts out for the lads. PSG were a different class, but no-one was really that bothered about the game. It was all about the trip, the booze, and the camaraderie really.

After the match there were a few scuffles with their Ultras, the Boulogne Boys, who were mostly sad looking skinheads, but this was very minor. The vast majority of the French fans were friendly towards us. Most of the fans then made for the red light areas of the Rue St Denis.

This was certainly an eye opener for all us Edinburgh lads. I'd seen a few prostitutes in Coburg Street in Leith, but nothing like this. A whole street full of them with many of them absolutely gorgeous. Also sex shops selling magazines on things that I didn't even know were possible! It was quite an education for a young lad and left me wishing that I hadn't wasted my time the previous night drinking with a gang of pissed up football fans and almost getting decapitated in the process.

I was much more worldly wise when I left Paris on the Thursday and on arrival back in London spent the night around Soho, which was a big let down after what I'd seen in Paris. It was a quiet night and we had a fairly early one to prepare us for the train home the next day.

\* \* \*

The best part of going away is coming home, and I had a night out on the Friday that would go down as one of the most infamous evenings in the history of the Edinburgh mod scene. The Westfield Bar, a fairly innocuous local pub with a function suite, just up from

Tynecastle, was staging a mod night. All my mates from the High Street mods were going, and trouble was widely expected as we knew a large contingent of scooter boys from Livingston were coming through as well.

We got up there fairly early and met up with a group of mods from East Calder that we knew quite well, and everyone set about having a good time. The atmosphere changed dramatically when the Livi mob came in though. Straight away there was tension and dirty looks flying about the place. As the drink flowed, the atmosphere deteriorated, and when one of our lot battered a Livi boy in the toilets it went off mental on the dancefloor, stools flying around as a 40 a side battle erupted. I don't actually know too much about what went on as I ended up on my back and had to wait a few minutes for the room to stop spinning before I could get up, with one side of my face expanding at quite a rate . . . that would be grief when I got home! It was ironic really. I'd gone all the way to Paris and come close a couple of times to getting done in, and eventually I come a cropper in a pub just five minutes from Tynecastle.

The battle, which Livingston had got the better off, had calmed down and the lights were back on as we got chucked out. Once out in the street, and with the Livingston lot going back to their coach, it all went off again. This time we got the upper hand, although by this time I was walking up the road with a couple of little modettes, milking the sympathy vote. The arrival of the police prevented the issue being settled there and then, and threats were issued by both sides to settle it at a mod night in Whitburn in a month's time.

\* \* \*

My next Hearts match was away at Dundee United on Wednesday, the 10th of October, in the second leg of the League Cup Semi Final. United had won the first leg at Tynecastle 2-1, so it was all or nothing on this game. We took a decent support of around 5,000 to Tannadice, and as usual took our place in the covered terracing right next to the segregation fence. By this time Dundee United had a decent sized mob of casuals, probably around 100 strong. We were still in single figures. As I had come up on a supporters bus, I hadn't seen any of their lot until I got into the ground. I was surprised by how many more they had since the last time we had been up there. I met up with the rest of the Hearts casuals next to the fence - all six of us. Needless to say, we were the subject of quite a lot of slagging from the United lot.

Unfortunately, it was not to be our night on the pitch as the home side dominated throughout and eventually ran out comfortable 3-1 winners. As the goals went in, the casuals on the other side of the fence became more lippy and soon the coins were flying between the two mobs. The police, who hated us after the trouble at Tannadice the previous season, weren't about to stand for any nonsense from us and they came in hard with the batons out. Hearts went mad and soon everyone was piling into the Old Bill. Funnily enough, the home fans seemed to go a bit quiet when all this was going on. The police retreated and contented themselves with a heavy presence in front of the Hearts section for the remainder of the game.

After the match, the United mob were waiting at the bottom of the hill that took us back to our buses. They had slapped a few Hearts fans who were just walking down, but the six of us had mingled in with the main body of the Hearts hooligan support who promptly steamed straight into the United mob. They may have all been dressers, but they were no match for the Hearts hooligans and they got battered everywhere.

On the Saturday, we had Dundee United again, at home in the league. I met up with the other casuals and this time we had about 15 boys. However, after the kicking they had got on the Wednesday, their firm didn't show. Just as well, as I'm not too sure what 15 of us would've done against around a hundred of them! Hearts took their revenge on the pitch with a comfortable 2-0 win which was much needed after our recent poor run of results in the league.

\* \* \*

The next day saw Paul Weller back in Edinburgh, as the Style Council played at The Playhouse. I met up with around 30 of the mods in The Royal Archer pub on the Sunday afternoon for the concert and also to get things sorted out for the trip to Whitburn the following week. We had got a 52 seater coach arranged and were confident of filling it mostly with blokes. We were out to slap them properly this time, but it wouldn't be easy. Whitburn was their manor and we could be well outnumbered through there. I offered to bring some of my mates from football along, but all credit to the mods who wanted to sort it on their own.

Anyway, back to the Style Council who were surprisingly good. Obviously not a patch on The Jam, but far better than anything else around at the time. The crowd was more mixed than it had been at Jam gigs, where it was usually about 90% Mod. For the Style Council, I'd say it was split fairly evenly between mods and normal punters. There were a few casuals in the crowd, and I clocked a little mob of three geezers all dressed in Fila in the bar. They looked over, but nothing was said. I naturally assumed that they must be Hibs lads, but I heard later that they were Aberdeen and that a few car loads of them had come down to see the band. They had in fact assumed that I was a Hibs boy as they didn't realise that Hearts had any casuals.

Around this time, Paul Weller had made a few comments that were favourable towards the casual movement. He had taken a great deal of interest in the style, and daubed us the mods of the Eighties, which we basically were. The original mod scene was all about quality clothing and fast changing fashions. Things that would be in one week would get you laughed at a couple of weeks later, and that is exactly what the original casuals were all about. Compare this with the mod revivalists who were continually looking back to the Sixties for their clothing, and there's nothing modern about that. Don't get me wrong, I thoroughly enjoyed my time as a mod, but I can see now how regressive it was. It did produce some great bands though.

The music of the casuals was also favourable to Paul Weller, with the strong northern soul following and the interest in modern soul and jazz funk. All of these styles were evident in the sound of the Style Council so it is no surprise really that the band attracted a casual following. In fact, the clothes that Weller himself was wearing around that time were total casual - Lacoste cardigans, Fila polo shirts, loads of gold bracelets and rope chains, and all topped up with the *Long Hot Summer* wedge haircut. Full on Scally.

Later that week, it was off to see The Pride play in the Waterloo Pub in Edinburgh. The band were gigging fairly regularly now and had moved away from having a mainly mod audience and into the mainstream. They were still pretty awesome live and looked to be on the verge of breaking into the big time, but like countless other decent bands before and after them, it sadly all came to nothing.

Friday, the 26th of October, 1984. The return leg of the Edinburgh versus Livingston battle at The Faces Scooter Club dance in Whitburn. Once again, we got out to the venue, which was on the main street in Whitburn, fairly early and soon got ourselves settled into one side of the room. The Livi lads came in and at first it looked as if there wouldn't be any trouble and the atmosphere began to calm a little as the two sides ignored each other. However, at the end of the night it all erupted. One of the Livingston had a go at a group of mods, which resulted in a small scale scuffle. We got outside and when the scooter boys came out we steamed into them. They stood and we had it toe to toe with them, right across the road. Coshes appeared from pockets and bottles were flying about. A geezer hit me with his crash helmet, but I managed to wrestle it off him and smacked him over the head with it. There was probably in excess of 100 blokes fighting in the street and we were drawing a sizeable audience of locals who seemed to be enjoying the show.

When the police turned up, they arrived two handed. It was hilarious watching those two coppers trying to stop over 100 blokes battling. They would break it up on one side of the road and when they moved away to try to stop it elsewhere, it would all flare up again. They were running back and forward like something out of the *Keystone Cops*. Eventually, all good things have to come to an end, and reinforcements arrived and they managed to break it up. As usual with police from small towns, they didn't want to make a lot of arrests because it's too much paperwork, and they were happy to send both lots home. In fact, they only made one arrest, which was my mod mate from the Elliotts gang.

After all, you have to make an example of someone. However, they did do him a favour in a way as he missed the boring 0-0 draw between Hearts and Hibs the following day!

So, that was it, between the Edinburgh mods and the Livingston scooter boys. It probably finished honours even and it certainly finished on a high, as I think everyone who was in Whitburn that night enjoyed the battle. Nowadays of course, there is no problems between the mods, scooterists and skinheads. Dwindling numbers in the three movements have made co-operation a necessity. However, before that would happen, there would be a few more run ins with other scooter clubs.

After the Hibs match, the next main Hearts game was at home to Celtic which saw us go down 5-1. An absolute nightmare of a game, and this would start a run of bad results which sparked some relegation fears just before Christmas. This was also the first game that I experienced a bit of anti-casual backlash from the rest of the

Hearts support. You would think that with the small number of us that we would have been invisible to the rest of the Hearts support, but no such luck! We were standing in the corner of the Shed in the section next to the choir, and after a bit of baiting between the two mobs, the scarfers steamed over to us and backed us out of The Shed into the School End terrace.

Obviously, after such a heavy defeat from Celtic there was a bit of boxing in Gorgie Road after the match. Just the usual sort of stuff, a couple of charges by Hearts, a few punches and bottles thrown, then the police moving in to split it all up. As I was walking along into Dalry Road with my mate, someone smacked me on the back of the head. At first I thought it was Celtic, but when I turned around there was about six or seven blokes in their late twenties, early thirties, all Hearts fans fronting us up with "come on you casual bastards."

It was a nightmare getting started on by your own fans. Luckily, before anything happened, a few Hearts scarfers that knew us and drunk in our local came over and were able to tell the blokes to fuck off as they knew them as well. So, as well as the opposition we were going to have to keep an eye on our own supporters as well. In fact, it was this "Jam Tarts and casuals don't go" attitude that prevented Hearts from getting the casual mob that they could've had. Too many people that couldn't cope with a change of fashion and the fact that we had stopped wearing colours. What possesses grown men to wear football colours anyway? It's ridiculous. Unfortunately, the caveman attitude was predominant and it became clear to any wannabe casual that Hearts should be avoided.

Hibs on the other hand had suffered no such resistance to the casuals, and as a result their mob was able to grow unobstructed. The balance of power in the city was beginning to shift towards Leith and the attitude of a large majority of the Hearts hooligan support was partly to blame for this happening. Their attitude ensured that in the early years, the Hearts casual mob would be one step behind the rest, and when eventually we did sort things out, it was a struggle to catch up with the main firms in Scotland, which would eventually be Aberdeen and Hibs.

Anyway, back to the Hearts - Celtic game. We made the papers after this, as Hearts were threatened with an appearance in front of the Disciplinary Commission after crowd trouble had erupted during the match and Davie Provan was hit by a coin thrown from the corner of The Shed. This Disciplinary Commission had been set up as a result of the riot by us at Easter Road earlier in the season. Provan apparently suffered bruising and a small cut to his forehead.

The next match of any significance was Aberdeen's visit to Tynecastle on Saturday, the 1st of December, for a game that Hearts lost 2-1. The Aberdeen mob was massive that day - we're probably talking about 2-300 strong. As I was on the bus to the match going along Princes Street, a lot of their young firm were all hanging around Princes Street Gardens. This mob numbered about 100 and at least half of them were wearing blue Kappa kagouls. It looked well cool, but there was a slight problem. I was also wearing a blue Kappa and I had a good chance of being taken for an Aberdeen fan by the Hearts support. Great!

In the game, I stood with about a dozen or so other Hearts casuals in the enclosure next to the Gorgie Road End. This area, despite being the nearest bit of home terracing to the away end, was populated by old men and their sons at that time, so there was no problem with our own supporters.

At first, the Aberdeen mob seemed curious to see a casual mob at Hearts, and we spent most of the match talking to each other at the fence. They were handing out newsletters and all that type of stuff that used to upset the media no end. One of our lads had been nicked before the match for handing out Hearts newsletters to Aberdeen boys as they queued up to get into the Gorgie Road End. *The Sun* newspaper and *Edinburgh Evening News* would eventually make a big thing about this incident as the lad came from a respectable middle class area of Edinburgh and had attended a public school. They tried to make out that he was the ringleader of the Hearts casuals, and as a result he ended up receiving a ban for what was a fairly innocuous offence. A good example of how the press were dealing with the "casual menace" at the time. Meanwhile, other fans who were arrested for engaging in running battles after the match were free to return to Tynecastle the following week if they wished. It was all a bit hypocritical.

As suggested, there was a substantial amount of trouble in the streets after the match. The 300 Aberdeen lads had laughingly been trying to arrange something with the 15 or so Hearts boys, but it ended up in a massive row between the Aberdeen casuals and the Hearts scarfers. The Aberdeen boys stood and had it with Hearts, and they steamed into us a few times, but in the end sheer weight of numbers had them backing off. There were running battles all the way along Dalry Road as Aberdeen made their way back to the station.

However, unlike most teams who go to Haymarket station on account that it's the closest to our ground and that all the trains to anywhere in Scotland have to go through Haymarket anyway, Aberdeen wanted to swagger through the centre of Edinburgh back to the Waverley Station. Me and two mates were standing at a bus stop opposite the Haymarket Bar when the 300 or so Aberdeen crossed over towards us, away from the station. There was no point in doing a runner as they had already spotted us. Our only saving grace was the fact that the police were with them. All their top boys came around us and gave us the come ahead, and we managed to mutter the usual stuff about there being too many police about. So the Aberdeen boys told us to get a firm sorted out and come along to the Waverley by 6pm. None of the other Hearts boys were around, and after a quick scout about we couldn't trace anyone, so decided that the best option was to go home. The odds weren't too attractive.

The following week we went to Ibrox, all ten of us. We got through to Glasgow pretty early and used the trip as an excuse for a shopping spree (even then, Glasgow had the better shops). Olympus Sports and a small sports shop called Greaves were the main targets, as some of the boys got their Kappa rain jackets . . . fashion leaders or what. We then had a few drinks and made our way down to Ibrox, where Hearts got a good 1-1 draw.

After the match, as we made our way back to Queen Street in the underground, we came across the fledgling ICF, or HMS (Her Majesty's Service) as I think they may still have been called then, who were about 15 strong. A few punches were thrown, then there was a short stand-off, but we ended up having a chat with each other about clothes and the casual scene in general.

The following Saturday we were away at Tannadice again. During the Rangers match we had sorted it out to go up there by train, and on the Saturday morning about 15 of us met up at Haymarket Station and boarded the Dundee train. It was a good laugh travelling with the boys, and all of us got on pretty well together, despite a few of the lads being younger and still at school. By the time we got to Dundee, the nerves had been building, and the old butterflies were going as the train pulled into the station. The adrenalin was pumping as we jumped down onto the platform and noticed that there were a few police hanging around for us. There were a few other Hearts fans on the train who were okay with us, and we all made it past the police no problem. As we got out of the station we separated from the other Hearts fans and made our way into the town centre. As we approached a footbridge, the United boys appeared and chucked a few bottles at us, but when we ran at them, they disappeared. First blood to Hearts.

All the lads old enough to do so went to the pub, while the younger boys waited outside. There wasn't any problems in the boozer and at about 2.30pm, we started to make our way to the ground. As we approached Tannadice, United appeared again. This time there were about 50 of them and they came charging down the road towards us. We stood for a bit, and were beginning to get slapped when the police intervened. Just as well because we would've been fucked. There was nowhere to run and we had to get through them to get to the ground. The police escorted us into the ground, where as usual we took up our positions right next to the segregation fence. There was a bit of abuse exchanged between the two mobs and the usual exchange of gifts flying back and forth. Mostly in our direction too, but nothing very heavy this time.

The game itself was dreadful, with Hearts getting turned over 5-2. Things were looking a bit bleak on the pitch so we'd have to do the business off the park. United weren't around immediately outside the ground, but they soon made an appearance on the long walk down towards the town centre and the station, and a few bottles were thrown at us. We backed off initially as they charged forward, but then stood our ground and a few punches were exchanged. We were outnumbered, and it looked bad for us until some Hearts scarfers who had travelled by train steamed in to help us, causing United to back off just as the police arrived and prevented any further trouble. We then had an escort back to the station, with United tailing us all the way.

Not as impressive a display as the main Hearts hooligan support had put on recently at Tannadice, but one that definitely earned us a bit of recognition. United were a well established firm by this time, and up until recently nobody even recognised Hearts as having a casual mob. Hopefully that perception would now be altered.

# Chapter Thirteen

The following Saturday we didn't have a game, so I met up with the mods in the Top Man Cafe on Saturday afternoon. They were going through to a mod dance in East Calder that night, had a bus organised, so I decided to go along. A nice quiet night out in sleepy East Calder, hanging around with your mates, and listening to some top sounds. What a laugh that was.

Whenever we set foot in the hall, it became apparent that not all the East Calder Mods were happy to see us there, with one younger bloke in particular trying to stir it. And after about a couple of hours in there, the inevitable happened. The East Calder lad had started getting lippy at one of our boys, so when he went to the toilet, some of our lot followed him in and done him. You could write the rest of the script yourself . . .

We made our way to the exit, gathering our mob together, as word went round the East Calder Mods about what had happened. The ones who had invited us through stuck by us though, as the rest of their mob got ready to have a go. We got outside, and stood and had it at the doorway as they had a pop. Despite them having the numbers, they were shit as their main boys stuck by us. The fighting spilled out onto the street, but it was all stop start stuff, as the main East Calder Mods were desperately trying to break it up.

The police turned up at that point and we were soon on our way back to Edinburgh. We'd done okay, but it wasn't over yet. They had organised another mod night in the Swiss Cottage in Edinburgh for just after the New Year. On our own manor, so we made plans to finish it properly there.

Christmas was good that year, with some more Fila items to add to the wardrobe. This would be the last time that sportswear (except trainers) would be bought for me, as the New Year would see Fila and Tachinni on its way out by the end of the season. I also got an Ellesse t-shirt which would last through the following summer as acceptable clothing, but the main item that Christmas was a crew neck jersey by Cerrutti 1881. This was at the beginning of the move in Edinburgh away from sportswear towards classic designer labels.

That Hogmanay, me and a mate from the scheme went up to The Tron to see the New Year in along with about 10,000 other people. This being before the New Year celebrations were turned into the winter version of the Edinburgh Festival that we have now. Despite the crowds, we managed to bump into a small group of the Hearts mob about ten strong, and a similarly sized group of Hibs casuals. Just as the bells began, a fight erupted between the two drunken mobs, but by the time the bells had ended, everyone was shaking hands, promising to "see each other" at the following day's Edinburgh derby.

January the 1st, the New Year's Day derby. It is an institution in Scotland, and it is definitely the game that all Edinburgh football fans miss the most when one of the Edinburgh sides is relegated. It's the most important of the derby matches to win for the fans because it can make or break the start to your year, but this time I am delighted to say, was a great start to 1985 for all the Hearts fans as we snatched a 2-1 win at Easter Road in front of 22,500. There were a few scuffles in the Dunbar End between Hearts fans and the police during the match, but on this occasion the violence was minimal, nothing like the full scale riot that erupted on that terrace during the match between the sides earlier in the season.

Again there was no trouble between the Hibs and Hearts casuals that I can recall, despite the previous night's ruck. Maybe this had something to do with the fact that our mob only numbered about 15 lads that day, with Hibs not having many more at that time. In fact, the only hostilities between the mobs that day was a few insults shouted at each other across the segregation fence . . . and that was more about slagging each other's choice of clothing than anything else. In reality, at the outset, Hibs and Hearts were very similarly dressed . . . probably due to the fact that all the casuals in Edinburgh shopped in Austin Reed's sports department.

Saturday, the 5th of January saw us at home to Dumbarton where an excellent display saw us dispose of The Sons 5-1. This, together with the victory over Hibs, helped to ease our relegation worries. Morton already looked to be down, and on their display that day at Tynecastle, it looked as if Dumbarton would be joining them. So, a good win coupled with a good performance had me looking forward to my night out at the Swiss Cottage that night, and I wasn't to be disappointed.

Everything that could go right about a night out occurred here. After the match, I had a couple of quick drinks in Gorgie and a pie supper, then caught a bus over to The Blue Blanket pub in the Royal Mile where the mods were meeting. Quite a few of the lads had turned up with their scooters, and after a couple of drinks I was able to get a lift out to the Swiss Cottage on the back of one. This meant that I was amongst the first five or six Edinburgh mods inside the club because the rest of the lads were coming by bus. This had the adrenalin pumping straight away, as we tried to look relaxed and natural as we walked up towards the bar.

The East Calder were already there when we arrived, and while most of the main ones were okay with us, the twat who had started all the trouble was there in the corner with a sizeable group of mates, giving us dirty looks. The organisers of the night explained to us that they had spoken to all their boys and apparently he had been assured by them that there would be no trouble, but we were sceptical about this - and quite right to be as it turned out. However, as more and more of our lot arrived in the club, we settled down to having a first class night out, and although East Calder still outnumbered us, it looked as if our turnout had deterred them from starting anything.

The music at the East Calder nights was always good, as unlike a lot of the pretentious Edinburgh nights where the DJs played soul and RnB only, the East Calder DJs mixed the soul and RnB with a good selection of Sixties beat and pop music and mod revival sounds. So, despite the tense atmosphere, we all spent a good chunk of the night on the dancefloor.

The percentage of girls at this night was quite high as well, and my main success of the night was spending about quarter of an hour in a cubicle in the ladies toilets with an East Calder Modette who was well tasty. I had seen her about a few times in Edinburgh, since she worked in a bank near to my work, and had fancied her for a while, so I was well happy at the way the evening was progressing. So no matter what the rest of the night held in store, I had got a result for Edinburgh.

Towards the end of the night, with everyone a bit pissed, some mouthing off started between us and their mob at the bar. This would probably have come to nothing if the DJ hadn't played *Down In A Tube Station At Midnight* by The Jam as his next record. Jam tracks are songs that are guaranteed to clear a dancefloor of girls and fill it with blokes, especially towards the end of an evening when everyone is pissed, so the scene was set with almost all the blokes in the club bouncing about the dancefloor. Testosterone overdose! I wasn't actually dancing, as I had sat with my new bird most of the night, trying to impress her as being a bit of a gentleman.

I don't think I was doing too badly either, but the next few minutes were about to undo a whole evening's work.

With all the jumping about on the dancefloor, the inevitable happened and it kicked off. The East Calder lads had been deliberately pushing into our firm, causing one of the Ferniehill Mods to retaliate (Ferniehill is a rough council estate on the southern fringes of Edinburgh). He was near the ringleader from East Calder who started squaring up to him on the dancefloor. The next thing the East Calder boy is flat on his back as my mate caught him square on the jaw. The whole dancefloor erupted, and bird or no bird, you have to stand by your mates. She was trying to stop me from getting involved, but gave up as I launched the chair that I was sitting on towards the East Calder side of the dancefloor, and then charged into the affray, smacking a couple of people.

The Edinburgh mods were going mad, and East Calder didn't want to know. Even their boys who were trying to break up the trouble were getting started on. The club was filled with the sound of girls screaming as the East Calder lads backed off into the corners of the club, leaving the twat who started the whole thing lying on the dancefloor. Needless to say, he took a severe kicking before we ran out of the club and into the night, just as the police were arriving. An excellent evening. A good booze up, good music, and a bit of sex and violence, and on your way home by the time the police arrive! And all that just after your team wins 5-1. What more could you ask for?

As for the girl, I saw her the following week coming out of the bank at lunchtime with her mates . . . and she blanked me.

Despite all that trouble, it wasn't to be the end of us going through to East Calder for mod nights. Their main organisers were all decent boys and they realised that the blame for both the lots of trouble should not be put on us. They sorted out their own troublemakers and they were nowhere to be seen in our future visits to East Calder. Anyway, they spoke with the Edinburgh mods and everything was taken care of and smoothed over.

Around this time, three of the biggest football riots in England erupted, which served to highlight the casuals in the media even more and brought a lot of new recruits into the movement. On the 13th of February, Chelsea were defeated 2-0 in the first leg of the League Cup semi-final at Sunderland. I had travelled down there with a mate to support Chelsea, and was taken aback at the level of violence displayed by the Chelsea fans at the end of the match.

Seats came flying out of the stand at the police and lumps of concrete were thrown from the terraces, before literally thousands of Chelsea fans went on the rampage through the streets of Sunderland. The Chelsea support was unbelievable that night. It consisted almost entirely of casuals, and there must have been around 6,000 of them.

However, this was just a warm up for the second leg at Stamford Bridge on the 4th of March. This time, Chelsea got beat 3-2, one of the Sunderland goals coming from an ex-Chelsea hero, Clive Walker. That was too much for some Chelsea fans to take, and someone ran on to the pitch and attacked Walker. There were various other pitch invasions during the game that night, and indeed one of Sunderland's goals was scored as a Chelsea fan was chased across the goalmouth by the police! When the fan was eventually caught and arrested, he was led away to a deafening chant of "Loyal supporter!" by a substantial number of Chelsea fans. The fans in the benches also ripped up the wood from the concrete and used them to attack the police, as substantial numbers spilled onto the running track and fought with mounted police to get onto the pitch.

After the match, there were serious running battles in Fulham Road as the police tried to get the frightened Sunderland fans out of the area. Further trouble erupted at Parsons Green as Chelsea fans ambushed a tube carrying the West Ham ICF back from a match at Wimbledon. A mental night which got substantial media coverage at the time.

The next game of any note at the football was when Hearts were drawn away to Brechin City in the Fourth Round of the Scottish Cup. We had beaten Inverness Caley in the previous round 6-0 at Tynecastle, and it was a fairly large travelling support of around 5,000 (total attendance, 6,250) who descended on the smallest town in Britain to have a senior football team. We completely took over the town, and hundreds of us bunked in over the hedge that served as a fence! Despite the terrific backing that we gave the team, their performance was absolutely dreadful, and we were lucky to get away with a 1-1 draw.

Apart from the 90 minutes of the game, it was a great day out. Brechin just seemed to be taken over by pissed up Jambos as the pubs did a roaring trade. There were a few casuals about (Dundee United, I think), but they kept well out of our way. Anyway, we got the expected win in the replay at Tynecastle with a "convincing" 1-0 win, which set up a home tie with Aberdeen in the next round.

In between the Cup games, there was a home match against Rangers which we won 2-0. The Rangers mob brought about 30 boys through for the game, and we had around 20 casuals on duty. The two mobs came across each other in front of the children's playground in Gorgie Road, and for a couple of seconds it looked as if it was going to kick off, but yet again the two firms had a chat with each other, although the atmosphere was more strained than it had been at Ibrox earlier in the season.

Saturday, the 9th of March, the day of the quarter final tie with Aberdeen, was also the day of a strange truce amongst Edinburgh casuals, as a lot of the main faces from Hibs came along with Hearts that day to have a pop at the ASC. The Hibs firm was really beginning to pull the numbers by now, and had started building a reputation that would eventually take them to the top. They no doubt saw Aberdeen as the firm to prove themselves against, and as a result were determined to take every opportunity to have a go at them.

As usual, a large firm of the ASC went to the Waverley station, instead of getting off at Haymarket, which was the nearest station to Tynecastle. The Aberdeen mob wanted to swagger through the city centre, and quite frankly they had gotten away with doing this previously, but this time Hibs were waiting for them. Whenever they left the station there was a series of incidents, and by the time the Aberdeen mob got to Gorgie, they had been involved in a fair few battles.

Inside the ground, the Hearts and Hibs mobs went into the enclosure, and stood right up at the fence, with Aberdeen on the other side. There were a few coins flying over the fence, and a couple of surges, but there were too many police around for anything serious to occur. It was a different story outside the ground after the game, however. The Edinburgh lads timed their exit from the ground perfectly so that they would hit the main Gorgie Road just as the Aberdeen escort went past.

When the two mobs saw each other, the police couldn't control it. Aberdeen came bursting through the escort and the Edinburgh mob surged forward. Result, total mayhem. A fair few Hearts scarfers got involved as well, and Aberdeen were soon backing off. Once again though, they didn't run, and tried their best to stand their ground when they could. The police managed to separate the fans by the time we got to Dalry Road, but it went off again in Shandwick Place, and again at the Waverley Station, although it was really only the Hibs mob who had tailed them as far as the Waverley. A great day out.

Anyway, after all that, Hearts drew 1-1, and the replay was set for the following Wednesday at Pittodrie. I went up there on a normal supporters bus, and got into the ground fairly early. Thousands of Hearts fans made the trip up, but were late in arriving due to traffic congestion. In the meantime, the Aberdeen police, thinking that Hearts hadn't showed up in numbers and faced with a near capacity crowd anyway, started letting Aberdeen fans who had been locked out of the home end into some empty sections in the away end. When our fans eventually turned up, they weren't allowed in, and scuffles broke out between Hearts and the police outside the ground. Inside it wasn't much better, with scuffling breaking out in the end, but when Hearts defender, Roddy MacDonald, was unfairly sent off for elbowing, and ten minutes later Aberdeen opened the scoring, the trouble escalated dramatically, and only the large police presence prevented a full scale riot. The game finished 1-0, and it was a angry Hearts support that left the ground, with more fighting with the police and clashes with Aberdeen on the way back to our coaches.

On the same night in the small town of Luton, an incident was unravelling that would keep Thatcher's latest victory in the EEC off the front pages of the tabloids, and would eventually cause her to try to tame the hooligans. The supporters of the infamous South East London club, Millwall, had travelled in numbers to Luton's Kenilworth Road ground for an FA Cup match. The fans were determined to outdo Chelsea's exploits against Sunderland, and over 10,000 of them arrived in Luton to find a town and a police force who were shitting themselves. The numbers travelling caught the police on the hop, and they tried to cram 10,000 into an end built for just 7,000 which obviously caused crushing. As there was space up the sides of the ground, a few Millwall fans jumped over onto the pitch to get into the seats, the police reacted, started to get a bit heavy, and the whole lot erupted.

The game was played in an extremely ugly atmosphere, and the Millwall fans' mood was not improved with their team's defeat at the hands of what the Millwall described as "a bunch of farmers". Their mood worsened when the police insisted on keeping them in after the final whistle for about 30 minutes, and they had basically had enough and had the numbers to do something about it.

The television pictures beamed across the world showed hundreds of young Millwall fans ripping out plastic seats, swarming onto the pitch, and bombarding the police with them, as the boys in blue ran for their lives. It was magic stuff. The Millwall boys were putting on a show, and football hooligans across Britain were loving seeing the police getting a bit of pay-back. A CSF newsletter that came out shortly afterwards congratulated the Millwall firm for a job well done at Luton.

I had another run in with Aberdeen on the 23rd of March when they were in Edinburgh to play Hibs. We were away at Dumbarton that day, and due to having a party to go to at night I hadn't bothered travelling. I was walking along Princes Street with some of my mod mates when I was surrounded by about eight Aberdeen boys, giving it, "Come on Hibs." Fists started flying and I had to do a runner through Jenners. Later that day, as the ASC made their way down Easter Road towards Hibs' ground, a heavily outnumbered Hibs firm confronted them, and after a brief skirmish had to back off.

Unfortunately, one of their number fell, and was set upon by the Aberdeen mob who almost kicked him to death. Luckily, after a few touch and go days, the guy survived and made a full recovery. It's been said before by others involved in the trouble, but nobody wants to see someone die because of football violence. Anyway, after this incident the news spread around Easter Road that a Hibs boys had almost died, and it was a huge Hibs firm that clashed with Aberdeen after the match. This would start the long and violent rivalry between the firms of Aberdeen and Hibernian.

That spring had seen the start of the quick fad hitting the casual movement. Looking back through the years there has been a lot of strange and awful fashions that caught on with the casuals for about a month or two. They would rapidly become 'must haves', then just as quickly descend into joke status. Those items included Pod sandals, Next bubblejackets, semi-flares, patent leather shoes and Farah slacks. However, the first of the strange items has to be the leather and suede patchworks that became popular in the winter of '84 and the spring of 1985. Aberdeen started wearing them around Christmas, 1984, and I saw them start to appear in Edinburgh (and indeed bought one myself) in January, '85. By March, April, everyone had them, and they were on their way out. They were strange looking things, and it's puzzling as to why they became popular. All our other gear was expensive, and designer, that's what it was all about. Patchworks, on the other hand, were cheap and nasty, and bought from cheapo shops in the Gallowgate in Glasgow.

The Pompey 6:57 Firm were renowned for wearing them in the autumn of '84, and some northern teams such as the Leeds Service Crew cottoned on around then as well. I can only presume that's where Aberdeen picked up on the idea from, and we followed on.

Gee2 knitwear was another strange one. Gee2 was a shop in Glasgow that became very popular amongst Scottish casuals, especially amongst Hearts. We became known as the Gee2 Boys. At the same time, Hibs were known as the Lacoste Mob. Obviously, Hearts also wore Lacoste and Hibs wore Gee2, but it was interesting to see how certain labels catch on better at different teams.

Anyway, back to the football. The final derby of the season was postponed on the 30th of March due to heavy snow, but that didn't stop an afternoon of running battles between Hearts and Hibs boys in the city centre. Unfortunately, we seemed to be doing most of the running. Hibs really started to get it together around this time, and they had the numbers with far more of their young support willing to adopt the casual image than was the case at Hearts. There were also a few Hearts lads for whom the violence was more important than the football, who started going with Hibs as they had better rows on their travels.

The game was played the following Tuesday at Tynecastle, and finished 2-2, after Hearts were 2-0 up. My memory of that last derby of the '84-'85 season was about 100 Lacoste alligators coming along at the head of the Hibs support after the match. There were a few scuffles with Hearts fans who were hanging around, but for the first time that I could remember, Hibs turned Hearts over in Gorgie.

After our poor showing on Tuesday, the Hearts firm bounced back for the game against Celtic at home on the Saturday. Even to this day, a Hearts - Celtic game is almost guaranteed to kick off at some point, and this match was no exception.

The best action was before the match. Around 40-50 of us were in the Haymarket Bar. This was us at full strength. We were all watching the station from the windows, and charged out of the pub when Celtic's mob, the Celtic Soccer Crew (or Roman Catholic Casuals, as it may have been at the time) came piling out at the head of their support. They were also at full strength that day with around 100 to 150 lads, and came charging towards us, chucking golf balls. We steamed in, and almost immediately Celtic backed off back into the station.

Their fans wanted to have a go as well, and as the police were sorting it out, fighting flared again. We done really well, as the Celtic fighting support topped 200 including their scarvers. There was further trouble along Dalry Road as the Celtic fans got an escort, but it really went off big again outside the Green Tree Pub (now Robertsons) in Gorgie Road, where running battles broke out that lasted off and on right up to the Gorgie Road terracing entrance. Celtic won the game 2-0 and there were a few small scale scuffles in Gorgie Road after the match, but nothing special as the police had it well sorted.

After the Celtic, we were away to Dundee, a game that I didn't bother travelling to, as the week after we all went to Ibrox. Hearts had a good firm for this match numbering around 40 to 50 lads, and there were a few scuffles with Rangers boys before the game. No talking to each other this time. However, the most trouble that day was on the Glasgow underground, as Hearts smashed up a carriage and fought with Rangers fans on the train. This was a typical end of season game, with neither side having anything to play for, and with a crowd of only 12,193 inside Ibrox, it wasn't exactly a highly charged atmosphere.

The following week we had a good turnout at home for the visit of Aberdeen, but they didn't really travel in numbers as they had already won the championship. However, that didn't stop it being an eventful day. During the first half, the casuals who now sat on the benches next to the segregation fence on the Wheatfield terrace, had suffered constant abuse from the scarfers in the corner. It was all the usual stuff . . . "Its magic you know, Jam Tarts and casuals don't go!", so nothing really to get worried about.

At half-time though, with the tension between the two groups heightening, the scarfers started giving it, "You're gonna get you're fucking heads kicked in!", and started walking towards us. All 50 or so of us stood up, turned towards them and fronted them up. Not one of them came near us. They got to about the halfway line and stopped. That was the Hearts scarfers last stand. The following season would see many of the faces in the scarfer mob joining the ranks of the casuals.

Our last game of the season was away at St Mirren. Around 2,000 Hearts fans turned up in a crowd of only 4,817. We had around 30 lads at that match, all up for a typical last day of the season drink up.  On arrival in Paisley we took up position in a bar near the station, and stayed there until about 2.30pm, before making our way to the ground.

St Mirren had the start of a casual mob by then as well, but there were only about ten or 15 of them at that time.  They would become a stronger force the following season and they were another mob to have a great name.  The LSD or Love Street Division, Love Street being the name of St Mirren's ground, was up there alongside the Saturday Service of Motherwell.  Anyway, we saw them before the match in the distance, but nothing happened, and we reached the ground pretty pissed.  In fact the whole Hearts support seemed to be pissed that day, and with the way the players went about their business, it makes me think that they had drunk a few too many as well.  There can be no other explanation for a 5-2 defeat . . . although the following season, St Mirren went one better, a result that was to cost us the championship in the end.

So, a pissed Hearts support and a shit display by the team could only result in one thing.  There was trouble on the Hearts terracing in the first half which the police had to come in to sort out.  At half-time there were further incidents, and towards the end of the match, our firm together with some Hearts scarfers left the ground, went round into the St Mirren end, and kicked it off, chasing them along the terracing.  The full time whistle saw the Hearts mob on the pitch with some of the other Hearts fans, before making our way back to Glasgow for a few beers before returning to Edinburgh.

The season finished with Hearts and Hibs in 7th and 8th place respectively, just above the relegation positions, but with a big enough points cushion for us not to worry too much.  Dumbarton and Morton were the teams to get relegated.

# Chapter Fourteen

The start of that summer gave us an example of football violence taken to its extremes when 39 Italians and Belgians died after a wall collapsed at The Heysel Stadium, Brussels, before the European Cup Final between Liverpool and Juventus. I remember watching the game at home and cheering on the Liverpool fans when they charged the Italians. After all, it was the Italians that had started the trouble and it was good to see the Scousers flying the flag when they scattered the Italians.

However, that all changed when the news reports of fatalities started to come through. As I've said before, no-one seriously wants to see someone lose their life because of football violence, and the Heysel disaster was definitely something that, coupled with a few other things, would see me pull away from the trouble eventually. Like most casuals around that time, I used to keep scrapbooks about football violence and casual fashion, but even although the Heysel disaster dominated the tabloids for days, I couldn't bring myself to collect the cuttings. Despite these feelings, I disagreed totally when the Liverpool fans were extradited years later to face manslaughter charges. It wasn't the Scousers that killed them, it was poor organisation by the authorities. The Belgians showed that they couldn't organise a piss up in a brewery, and this together with a stadium that was failing to bits, were the main contributors to the disaster. Also, if the Italians had stood to finish what they started, it would have been a different story altogether.

The rest of the summer of '85 saw Edinburgh go casual and we soon become public enemy number one. There were newspaper articles telling parents how to tell if their son was a casual, and every pisshead in town seemed to be up for a row, "Wi' they Casual bastards". Going into large parts of Edinburgh also suddenly became dodgy with the emergence of casual street gangs in every housing estate, and for the next year or two there was almost constant gang warfare which on top of the battles between Hearts and Hibs made Edinburgh a very violent city.

Those gangs sprung up everywhere, from respectable Murrayfieid (the Tufty Club) and Orchard Brae (Orchard Football Trendies), to the estates of Gracemount (Gracemount Baby Crew), Gilmerton (Hyvots Dressers), Wester Hailes (Wester Hailes Casual

Crew), Muirhouse (Muirhouse Casual Firm), to inner city areas such as Saughton with the Saughton Chosen Few, nowhere was spared. In some areas of Edinburgh, the violence became an almost nightly occurrence during the summer months. For example, gangs from Gracemount, Gilmerton and The Inch clashed frequently along the Lasswade Road, with petrol bombs being used by Gracemount during one brawl with The Inch.

There were also battles in sleepy Crammond, as Gracemount's mob would visit on a Sunday to clash with Muirhouse, and outlying towns around Edinburgh such as Musselburgh, Penicuik, and Peebles were visited by Gracemount, usually on their Gala Days. It was like a re-run of Edinburgh in the 1970s when gangs such as The Young Leith Team, Young Gillie Team, Young Clery Derry, and the Young Lochend Shamrock, to name a few, would fight on a regular basis, although it was a lot worse in the Seventies when you take into account the battles between the mods, punks and skinheads.

In fact, Edinburgh had a violent street gang culture stemming back from the hard mods and skinheads of the Sixties and early Seventies, so it was difficult to see why all the fuss was being made about the casuals. Up until the late Eighties, every generation of teenagers has had their own version of gang culture. The only thing that changed was the fashions.

As well as the housing estate mobs, or Chippy Casuals as they were known because they were always found hanging around their local chip shops, both Hearts and Hibs attracted a lot of youngsters who were turned on by the casual image. These were schoolkids who knew nothing about Ben Shermans, Doc Martens, and US Army parkas, but knew everything about the latest street gear from the Italian designers such as Armani, Fila, and so on. The youngsters formed their own little mobs called Baby Crews, and with Hibs having the bigger firm, they also attracted a sizeable Baby Crew. The Hibs manager at the time was John Blackley, and the Hibs kids named themselves the BBC, Blackley's Baby Crew, although I'm not sure if John Blackley would have appreciated the honour!

The BBC hung around in Princes Street and in particular outside the Wimpy (now Burger King) at the junction of Princes Street and Castle Street, and the "pulling up'" and on occasions "taxing" (taking newly bought clothes from individuals as they left a shop) happened on a more regular basis. Whilst the BBC was essentially a football mob, during the summer they would go on tour around the different areas of Edinburgh, like the Gracemount mob, to take on the local street gangs.

The rest of the summer was spent buying clothes for the new season. Diadora trainers were still in as footwear, and stonewashed jeans had now replaced bleached jeans totally. Cords were still popular and you could get away with some sports shirts such as Ellesse. However, the casual must have at the start of the new season was a paisley pattern shirt with a long tail. Worn outside of the stonewash jeans with a pair of Diadoras on, top button fastened, it looked the business, especially when a small metal Hearts badge was pinned on the front. Total casual. Some lads used to wear a cameo broach at the top button, but I never got into that myself. Burberry golf jackets also got big that summer in Edinburgh. The famous checked scarf had been worn extensively the previous winter and now it was onto the jackets. Burberry would become one of THE classic labels of the casual movement.

There were a couple of good gigs that summer as well. The Style Council played the last ever gig in the Glasgow Apollo (it was demolished the following day) on Sunday, the 16th of June. I went through with a mate who was a skinhead to find that the vast majority of the crowd at the concert were mods. To say the two of us got a few funny looks is an understatement. Apart from that, the gig was superb as usual.

Another gig worth a mention was mod band, Makin Time, at the Minto Hotel. An excellent night which was bettered by me smacking a leading London mod who was with the band. He had done me out of money for records about four years earlier. Revenge is sweet.

# Chapter Fifteen

The 1985/1986 season . . . the season that would promise so much and eventually break our hearts, and unfortunately a season that would see the bandwagon jumpers turn up at Tynecastle and start their process of diluting and eventually almost killing off the atmosphere at Tynecastle.

Hearts spent their pre-season in Germany, playing against some low scale opposition from the German Oberligas and Regionaligas, and then it was back to Scotland for the Premier League opener against Celtic at Tynecastle. The numbers of casuals that Hearts had for this game was quite impressive. The firm was now around 150 strong with many new faces turning out, having learned the lesson the previous season that the casual look was the way forward. Celtic arrived at Haymarket around 2.15pm, about 250 of them, but the police had also learned a few lessons from the previous season, and there was no chance of getting anywhere near them at Haymarket, the police nicking anyone that hung around.

The Celtic mob were taken along Dalry Road and Gorgie Road with a huge escort, with the Hearts mob walking on the other side of the road, trying constantly to cross over to mingle in, but without much success. However, our patience eventually paid off. As the Celtic mob stood in the queues to get into the Gorgie Road End terracing, we managed to get through the police to have a pop at them. It probably lasted all of a minute, if that, but it was enough to get the adrenalin pumping for the game.

Just under 22,000 were in Tynecastle to watch a cracking match, where Hearts went 1-0 up with a goal from ex-Celt, John Colquhoun, but then let in a last gasp equaliser to Celtic. Little did we realise the significance that goal would have come the end of the season.

Outside the ground after the match, it is always easier to get away with having a row as the policing at Tynecastle has never tried to keep the fans segregated, and instead just let's everyone mingle on Gorgie Road. The Celtic mob, who had got a lot of abuse in their own end from their own fans during this match, again had a large police escort, although this was probably as much to stop them fighting their own fans as it was to keep the two rival casual gangs apart. There were a few scuffles in Dalry Road, but they amounted to little more than fronting each other up, with a few punches thrown. There were too many police around to get away with anything else.

After Celtic were put on their train, we had a few drinks and got it sorted for the following week's match at St Mirren, arranging a train and leaving time. After a few drinks, the lads all went off on their own - staying in a mob for the whole Saturday evening hadn't started yet.

The following week at work dragged slowly by as I was constantly looking forward to mobbing up the next weekend. The excitement had come back into football, and we were starting to get a good little firm together. It was the excitement of being into something at the start. This season would be the height of the casual movement in Scotland, and I was exactly the right age to get into it properly. Although I was a mod in 1979 at the height of the revival, I was still quite young, and as such wasn't able to participate fully. This time I was the right age to get into the whole casual thing properly.

At last, Saturday arrived, and it was good to see about 70 of us were making the trip through to Love Street. When we arrived in Queen Street Station, Glasgow, there was a welcoming committee waiting for us. Celtic had around 100 lads in and around the station, and it was all off straight away as soon as we got off the train. As usual, the police were quick to arrive on the scene, but this brief scuffle gave us a taster of what it would be like from now on in Glasgow. Irrespective of whether we were playing one of the Glasgow sides or merely passing through, whoever was at home in Glasgow would try and pick you off.

This was bad news when you were going to somewhere like Clydebank and we didn't have many with us, because the Glaswegians were always in numbers, and more often than not, were tooled up as well. Anyway, the police cleared the station of Celtic, and we went for a look at some of the Glasgow shops. While we were walking around the city centre, the Celtic mob had another pop at us which resulted in a leading Hearts boy getting a bottle across the head and being rushed to hospital. Whilst he was waiting for treatment, two Celtic boys arrived in casualty with stab wounds.

While our mate and a couple of his close friends went off to hospital, the rest of us made our way to Central Station for the train to Paisley, home of St Mirren. On arrival, it was far more on top than it had been a few months previously. Like ourselves, the LSD had gained a lot of new recruits over the summer, and when we got off the train, we could see their scouts, some younger kids, running out of the station to tip off their main mob that we were here.

As we emerged from the station, we could see St Mirren already teaming up and then we were charging at each other. They had the numbers on us, but the vast majority of them didn't really want to know that day, and they started backing off. First blood to us, as the police arrived to give us an escort to the ground. The match itself was dreadful, as Hearts crashed 6-2. I didn't think that it could get any worse than the previous season, but you can always rely on Hearts to let you down just that little bit more.

As we left the ground after the match, their firm had come round to our end, and it went off again almost straight away. This time the LSD were badly outnumbered as a lot of Hearts scarfers got involved as well, and it was an eventful trip back to the station, with some dodgy moments as the bottles started to fly through the air. When we got back to Central, we started to walk towards Trongate, to meet the oncoming Celtic fans, and there were a few more scuffles before the police split it up and gave us an escort back to Queen Street.

When we got back to Edinburgh, a few of us went up to the Southside Snooker Centre Bar, where we met up with two or three Hibs lads who were mates and who also drank up there. Over the weeks, this would be a meeting place on a Friday and Saturday night for an increasing number of Hearts boys, although it was never exclusively Hearts and there were always a few Hibs around. It was more a group of mates having a drink rather than a football mob.

Unfortunately, the word got around that it was a Hearts meeting place, and as a result it was visited by groups of Hibs lads from time to time, and although serious trouble never really broke out (due to the fact that there were always Hibs lads with us), it came close a few times. We would continue going to the Snooker Centre into the spring of the following year, but then we started to drift away to another local pub when a change of scenery was required.

At that match, I bought an item of clothing that was to be another quick casual fad that would last about a couple of months then fade away. A half and half ski hat. Souvenir sellers had recently started taking the bobbles off the traditional football bobble hat and converting them into ski hats. Most of the plain Hearts ones were worn by your every day fan, but the ones that the casuals wore were split half and half with an English team. I got a Hearts /

Chelsea ski hat, which I think I only wore on one occasion. It was more a thing to have than to wear.

On the following Tuesday, we had a League Cup match up at Links Park, Montrose. We knew that Montrose had a little mob, calling themselves the Montrose Soccer Unit (they later changed their name to Portland Bill's Seaside Squad). There were also a few Aberdeen lads from the Montrose area, so we knew that it would be worth travelling the 90 odd miles to get there.

Montrose is a hard place to get to on a service train in midweek, so a few of the boys went up on a football special that BR were running, and the rest of us went up on a supporters bus. Before the game, we never saw any of their boys, but once in the ground they had a little mob, about 30 to 40 strong up at the segregation fence. Hearts had around 15 to 20 tops, including a leading Hibs lad who had come up with a Hearts mate. This grabbed the attention of the Aberdeen lads in the Montrose end, who wasted no time in letting everyone know that they knew he was a Hibs boy. Nothing really happened inside the ground, except a little bit of pushing and shoving at the segregation fence, which ended up as a stand off with the police.

There weren't many Hearts fans there, and the game itself was pretty predictable with Hearts running out 3-1 winners. After the match it went off straight outside the ground. The MSU had come round to our end, and scuffles broke out straight away. The police pushed them back down the road, and we tried to have a go back as a few bottles came over at us. We got back to our buses, but I believe Montrose tried to have another go at the mob who went on the train while they were being escorted back to the station.

While we were at the match that night, I think every casual there would have had their videos set to record a documentary on TV called *Hooligan*. The documentary, which looked at the activities of West Ham's infamous Inter City Firm, would become legendary in casual circles, as important to the casual movement as *Quadrophenia* was to the mods. The programme showed West Ham having a go at Spurs at Upton Park, and then away at Sheffield Wednesday. It also showed them, rather embarrassingly, getting turned over at home by Chelsea, and slapped up at Manchester United, but the best footage was of the Millwall lads at the battle of Kenilworth Road.

The following Saturday, we were away at Ibrox, where we went down 3-1 in front of 35,500. Hearts had around 3,000 there, with about 100 of us casuals making the journey. There wasn't a reception for us at Queen Street, but when we came out at the Ibrox underground station, they were there in numbers. Hearts done okay in the ensuing battle, but in reality came off second best. It was a different story after the match though.

We all left a few minutes before the final whistle, and made our way round to the back of the main stand. The Rangers mob, who had been in the Enclosure, came out early as well, and we charged into them. They backed off, and when we charged again they ran up towards the Copeland Road End. By this time, a lot of Rangers fans were leaving the ground as there was only about a minute left, and a few of them got involved as well. We were outnumbered, but stood our ground, and eventually the police steamed in and took us around to the underground and put us on a train. It was well dodgy for us at Ibrox that day, but we got away with it being about honours even. However, the next trip to Ibrox would be a terrifying experience.

# Chapter Sixteen

One of the best things about going to Hearts in the Seventies and early Eighties was the atmosphere in the ground. An atmosphere that is all too often absent today. A situation which was occurring even before they knocked the terraces down. Nowadays, you are guaranteed a good atmosphere for Celtic, Rangers and Hibs when they visit Tynecastle, but as for the rest, forget it. Yet this is the same ground that used to provide so much atmosphere when we had only 4,000 in the stadium for a match against Berwick! What has gone wrong?

Despite the bigger crowds and the advent of more families attending (I won't say the return of the families because, even before the trouble started, football was never a game for families - Fathers and sons, yes, but families, no), football is on its last legs. The families are turning it into something no different from any other spectator sport. What made football stand out from the rest was the pure passion that the fans showed. Okay, this passion often involved bad language and trouble, but it's what made the game different. That's not to say everyone should condone trouble, but the campaign to clean up the game will probably (ironically enough) end up killing it.

The people who run the clubs and the players and officials are now working to different agendas. The authorities and the chairmen cannot see further than the next big earner. Fill the ground with families because they spend more. More on refreshments and more on the all important merchandise. This is all occurring at a time when the players and managers are complaining about the lack of atmosphere in the grounds. Well you can't have it both ways. It's either families OR atmosphere. Lads, geezers, whatever you want to call them, are the people who create atmosphere, not women and children. But with lads you will get bad language and on occasions trouble.

Suddenly all of the newcomer families are urging the authorities to squeeze out of the game the very people who stood by football in general, and Hearts in particular, when they should have been paying us to watch, not the other way around.

Now, I'm not saying that there is no place for women and children, or even easily offended people at football. It's more about making a point that the real football fans are often the most undesirable ones in the eyes of the authorities. Unfortunately in Britain, the powers that be and the media have stigmatised the football fan to such an extent that it's like a witch hunt now. The hooligan problem has largely died off on its own anyway, but the witch hunt is still in full flow. Swearing will be the next thing to be banned. Why can't the people who are in charge realise that there can be a place inside football grounds for everyone? The Italian authorities are able to handle this concept where large areas of their grounds are reserved for rowdy fans (Ultras as they call them), while the rest can watch the match in peace in the other parts of the stadium. The atmosphere can be enjoyed by everyone without having to experience it close up unless you choose to.

Of course, the other reason for the lack of atmosphere is down to the kids of today. Maybe I'm just getting old, but as far as I'm concerned, most of them don't have a fucking clue. As you can see from this book, it was all about going to the match with a group of your mates, and standing with like minded people once you got there. Fashion, music, and football, the whole lot was interlinked. It was called terrace culture. Two brothers from Watford are now making a fortune, churning out books on the subject. Maybe more of today's youngsters should read them.

Of course, maybe we shouldn't expect anything different from the generation who have succeeded in killing off Britain's most successful export of all time, the youth cult. From the Fifties to the Eighties, we've had teds, mods, skinheads, glam, boot boys, punks, casuals, and plenty more besides, as the youth of Britain led the world. Now there's nothing. Just a bunch of kids who want to copy the fashions of the most clueless country in the world, the USA.

Maybe a new generation will come through with different ideals, and they may create their own football culture. Let's hope so, because it's about time that we sang a wider variety of songs than *The Hearts Song*, and *Hello! Hello!*. There has been a few good ones recently, with the European song being a personal favourite, but not enough people sing it. Here's some others from the not too distant past that may bring back a few memories . . .

We've got Bobby Bobby Prentice on the wing, on the wing!
We've got Bobby Bobby Prentice on the wing, on the wing!
Bobby, oh Bobby Prentice, oh Bobby Prentice on the wing!
Bobby, oh Bobby Prentice, oh Bobby Prentice on the wing!

I'm forever blowing bubbles,
Pretty bubbles in the air,
They fly so high, nearly reach the sky,
Then like the Hibs, they fade and die,
Rangers always running, Celtic running too,
We're the Gorgie Boot Boys,
And we're running after you!

The Celtic throw bottles
And the Rangers throw cans,
But they run like fuck,
From the mental Hearts fans!

Bertie Mee said to Bill Shankly
Have you heard of the North Bank Highbury,
Shanks said no I don't think so,
But I've heard of the Gorgie . . . Aggro!

We had joy, we had fun,
We had (Celtic, Rangers, Hi-Bees - take your pick) on the run,
But the fun didn't last,
cos the bastards ran too fast.

Away the lads,
You should've seen them running,
Running down the Easter Road,
Because The Shed was coming,
All the Gorgie Boys, with their Docs and their braces,
Running down the Easter Road, to smash their fuckin' faces.

We're going up, you're going down,
We're gonna wreck your fuckin' town!
We're gonna rape, we're gonna pillage,
We're gonna wreck your fuckin' village!

All I need is a walking stick,
A hand grenade, and a council brick,
A Celtic fan, to punch and kick,
We are the Gorgie . . . Boot Boys!

The Northern Lights Of Aberdeen,
Mean sweet fuck all to me,
The Northern Lights Of Aberdeen,
Mean sweet fuck all to me,
I've been a Hearts fan all of my life,
And many a sight I've seen,
But the Northern Lights Of Aberdeen
Mean sweet fuck all to me!

We are mental, we're insane,
We cause trouble at the football games
With a M-A-N, 0 and R ,
We are the mental . . . Manor!

# Chapter Seventeen

Anyway, back to the football. The next game, after Rangers, was the first Edinburgh derby of the season at Tynecastle. As I've said previously, Hibs were really pulling huge numbers into their firm by now, and this coupled with a good number of very game lads and excellent organisation meant that in a short period of time they had become one of the main forces in Scotland. The previous autumn it would have been unthinkable for Hibs to come over to Tynecastle and turn us over, but after their turnout at the last derby of the previous season, we knew that this was a very real threat.

As well as the above facts about Hibs, the main advantage they had over us was the fact that they hung out in the city centre. This meant that a lot of Hearts boys were reluctant to put themselves up against Hibs because it meant grief at a later date, maybe on your way to work, or when you were out with non-football mates, or a girl. It ended up getting really silly in the town. Of course, Edinburgh wasn't the only city where violence between local rivals became ongoing for seven days a week, 24 hours a day. You only need to read the excellent book, *Football Hooligans - Knowing The Score*, by Garry Armstrong, which deals with Sheffield United's Blades Business Crew for proof of that. A large part of this book chronicles all the street battles in the city with Wednesday lads away from football. However, the book also mentions periods of truce, where the two mobs could inhabit the same city centre pubs without trouble erupting. That scenario never occurred in Edinburgh.

Anyway, on the day of the match, Hearts mobbed up at Haymarket around The Haymarket Bar. There was an okay turnout of around 100 to 150 lads, so we felt confident enough. Then Hibs turned up around 2.15pm with around 200. Hearts came out of the pub and had a go, with the police, who had been keeping an eye on the Hibs mob, stepping in to break things up before it really got started. We had done fairly well there, but unfortunately came unstuck in Gorgie Road when a charge by the CCS had Hearts backing off.

After the match, which we won 2-1, the Hibs mob once again marched at the head of their support along Gorgie Road. There were a few scuffles along the way, but nothing of much note, as the police once again kept the two sides apart. If anything, the coming of the casuals made it easier for the police to control crowds once the Old Bill had sussed it out. Previously at a Hearts - Hibs game, trouble could have erupted anywhere and involved anyone, but now the police knew exactly where the trouble would come from. Also, previously when trouble erupted, loads of people, not necessarily hooligans, would join in, but now, with the Hearts fans' attitude towards casuals, this was unlikely to happen, so the amount of possible participants was drastically reduced too.

That night in Edinburgh, there were a succession of running battles, as the CCS came back down to Haymarket looking for Hearts. There was also disturbances between rival gangs of casuals in Lothian Road.

After Hibs, there were two away games at Aberdeen (one in the League Cup and one in the Premier), but as Pittodrie was being done up at the time, there was a very limited amount of tickets for away fans, so none of us bothered going up. That away match would keep until later in the season.

The next away game of note was on the 21st of September at Motherwell. As mentioned previously, the Motherwell firm, the Saturday Service, was well respected, and as a result we took quite a good number through by train. Probably about 150. As we were changing trains in Glasgow, it kicked off with Rangers in Central Low Level, and also outside Central Station, but that was it before the match as nothing happened when we arrived in Motherwell.

However, when we got into the ground, a leading Hibs lad phoned through a bomb scare, and the police evacuated the Motherwell and Hearts fans from the covered terracing onto the pitch, where minor scuffles broke out. After the all clear, and as the fans were making their way back into the terracing, both mobs charged each other on the pitch, but the police managed to get in between them. After the match, there were running battles with Motherwell on the way back to the station, which Hearts got the better off.

The following week saw us through in Glasgow again for our away trip to New Kilbowie Park, Clydebank. Surprisingly, we had a good mob again, about 200 strong this time, and on arrival in Glasgow the older lads went for a drink in The Berlin Bar, outside Queens Street, whilst the baby crew raided a fishing shop and nicked loads of deerstalkers. You then had the ridiculous sight of loads of Hearts lads wandering around with deerstalker hats on.

Anyway, Rangers were at home to Aberdeen that day, and while we were in the pub, a firm of Aberdeen came out of Queen Street and steamed straight into a large mob of Rangers who suddenly appeared. It went off mental right outside the pub that we were drinking in. After watching for a minute or so, Hearts came out of the pub and got involved as well, resulting in a three way fight, and the police were in big trouble trying to control it. Pure adrenalin buzz.

The down side came as the police began to restore order. Hearts were all split up, and a mob of around 20 of us ended up trying to get into Central Station Low Level at the same time as around 100 ASC. They were giving it to the police that we were "Aberdeen as well", and we nearly got pushed in amongst them, but thankfully, we managed to get away with it.

Nothing happened once we got through to Clydebank, although the regular Hearts support did give us a few strange looks when we walked into the ground with our deerstalkers on. The game was awful, with Hearts losing 1-0 in front of a crowd of around 3,500 (about 2,500 of whom were Hearts). We were expecting a repeat of what had happened earlier when we got back to Glasgow, but we were to be disappointed as the Rangers - Aberdeen game had been held up for around 15 minutes due to fighting in the Rangers end, and the two firms weren't back in the city centre when we arrived. In fact, the police had things well under control by then because the ASC got a foot escort all the way back to Queen Street, and the police put us on our train to Edinburgh before they had reached the station to be packed off back to Aberdeen.

Our next game was against Dundee at home, and they caught us on the hop. By then, the two Dundee mobs were pooling their resources, and their Utility Firm could turn up at either Dens Park or Tannadice. As Hibs were at Dundee United that day, we thought that the Utility would stay at home for Hibs, so when around 100 of their boys got off at Waverley and walked past the Haymarket, Hearts were all over the place and Dundee got the result. After the match, Hearts got it together a bit better and tailed them along Dalry Road, eventually running them when they came out of their escort just before going into Haymarket Station.

So, not a bad start to the season for us, but a pity the team hadn't started so well. We'd had a few dodgy times against Hibs, Rangers and Dundee, but overall hadn't done too badly. However, the next game, Celtic away, would be our best to date.

# Chapter Eighteen

Any game against Celtic is a good one for the Hearts hooligan. Even now, it is probably still the fixture which sees Hearts causing the most trouble. As well as the obvious sectarian differences between a large number of the fans, there is the added Edinburgh - Glasgow rivalry.

During the casual years, the fighting between the teams was pretty heavy. A trip to Parkhead would guarantee the largest turnout of Hearts casuals for an away game for two or three seasons. As well as their mob, most of the normal Celtic scarfers hated us too, and they always seemed to be up for a row. The scene was set.

On the 12th of October, 1985, Hearts took a mob of around 250 through to Glasgow. It was unbelievable at Haymarket that morning when we saw the firm that we had. We all travelled through on the same train, and when we arrived at Queen Street and the British Transport Police saw what we had, they were on their radios straight away. Celtic were waiting outside in George Square with around 150 lads, and a mass charge into the Square sent them scattering. Running battles broke out down a few of the side streets, and for what seemed like absolutely ages, it was pure mayhem.

The following day's *Sunday Mail* described the incident as follows . . . 'Shoppers scattered when rival fans clashed in Glasgow City Centre before the Celtic - Hearts match. Police reinforcements raced to the scene as groups of fans fought a running battle in George Square. No-one was injured, but seven fans were arrested. "We had the city centre well policed and the trouble was quickly contained," claimed a police official . . . ' Says it all really.

Eventually the police swamped the area and sorted out an escort to take us on foot to Parkhead. As we approached Trongate, Celtic showed again and scuffling broke out, but it was quickly dealt with by the police. For the rest of the journey, Celtic pelted us with missiles as they tried to get at us and we tried to break through the escort. As we got near the ground, a lot of their regular supporters had joined in as well - so much for Celtic and casuals don't go! Their mob now was probably around 500 strong, and although there were plenty of scuffles, the mounted police managed to keep the fans apart for most of the time.

At the match, Hearts won 1-0, courtesy of a John Robertson goal. Robbo was later carried off with a neck injury. This win was very much against the run of play, with Celtic pounding the Hearts' defence constantly throughout the game, and as a result, there were numerous angry Celtic fans waiting outside for us.

As we firmed up and started to walk back to the station, Celtic came at us with missiles, and Hearts backed off initially before charging back. Again, loads of their fans got involved and it was going off all over the road when the police arrived and sorted out an escort once again for us. On the way back to the city centre, it was a repeat performance of the journey to the ground, with Celtic trying to get at us, hurling missiles as they did so. I got hit on the head with a coin which brought a smirk to the face of one of the coppers escorting us.

Due to the numbers of police, there were no further battles and we were led into Queen Street by our escort via the taxi rank and side entrance, where we were made to line up before being searched. We then had our photos taken and were put straight onto an awaiting train. A top day out, as per usual, to Parkhead.

Meanwhile back in Edinburgh, Hibs were entertaining Aberdeen, in what was a bit of a grudge match after the serious attack on the Hibs lad by Aberdeen the season before. Hibs had a huge firm that day and basically caned Aberdeen all over. As the ASC were being taken back to the Waverley, Hibs attacked Aberdeen once more and a petrol bomb was thrown into the middle of Aberdeen's firm. Mental when you think of it, a petrol bomb in Princes Street at 5.30pm on a Saturday evening. The casuals were certainly making the news that weekend.

On the pitch, Hearts were beginning to string the results together, and we easily beat St Mirren 3-0 the following Saturday. The Buddies never brought any boys through so there was no trouble at the match. Afterwards, a few of us went out drinking in Newington, which eventually led to us gatecrashing a student party in Dalkeith Road. Needless to say, there were numerous disturbances at the party and the police were called to break it up.

Strange as it may seem now, clothes from Next became very fashionable with the casuals around this time. The Next chain was just beginning to appear on the high streets with their selection of better quality chain store clothing. In fact, one of their jackets was to become a huge casual must have. Called the bubble jacket, it was basically just a baggy zip-up canvas / cotton hooded jacket. It's hard to see why they were so popular, but everyone got into them.

There was no match for us the following Saturday. Our game against Aberdeen was postponed because they were playing Hibs in the League Cup Final the following day. Aberdeen won 3-0, and not surprisingly, there was severe disorder outside Hampden after the match as hundreds of Hibs boys went on the rampage, running Aberdeen and attacking the police.

Anyway, on the Saturday, I went through to Glasgow shopping, got another Gee 2 jumper and the Next jacket. It was a bit of a dodgy thing to do now, go shopping in Glasgow, as you could literally turn the corner and walk into a mob numbering hundreds. There were a few close calls, but as I was on my own, I managed to stay inconspicuous.

* * *

The following Wednesday we played Aberdeen and beat them 1-0, which was a great result for us. With it being a midweek match, there wasn't many Aberdeen boys at the game, but there was still not a bad turnout of around 50 casuals. Hearts probably had around 100. I don't remember seeing any trouble before the match, and after the game, the Edinburgh police, who were very edgy after the petrol bomb incident at Hibs, made sure that the ASC got a heavy escort back to Haymarket.

On the 2nd of November, it was another trip to Dundee for a 1-1 draw with United. I can't actually remember much about this game, as all trips to Dundee back then seem to merge into one. It was fairly predictable whenever we went there. Walking back into town after the match while Dundee and Dundee United casuals charged down side streets at you. What I do remember is an incident that occurred in Edinburgh that night when we bit off a bit more than we could chew.

A few of us from the South Side Snooker Centre, Hibs and Hearts, had gone over to Morningside for a drink. As we walked past The Merlin Pub, there were a few blokes who started fronting us up. As we stopped to have a go, loads more piled out of the pub, and scattered us. They were YMBO lads (Young Mental Bar-OX) and not to be messed with. It was well on top that night.

On the 9th of November, it was the second derby match of the season at Easter Road. The night before we were sitting in the Snooker Centre having a quiet drink, and Hibs came in mob handed. It didn't actually kick, but it was a bit of a heavy atmosphere. The

109

only reason that it didn't go off was because there were a couple of Hibs lads drinking with us.

The next day over 100 Hearts met up at Haymarket, and we were going to get the train to Waverley to surprise Hibs by arriving unexpectedly. Unfortunately, Hibs came up to Haymarket looking for us just before we were about to get the train, and a major battle erupted outside the station. Hearts done very well in this incident. Hibs, who had the numbers, initially chased Hearts into the station, but we charged back out, and it went back and forward a couple of times, with traffic cones flying about and office workers standing at of their windows watching, before the police split it up. It finished roughly honours even. There were a couple of Manchester City lads with Hearts that day who seemed to enjoy themselves.

That turned out to be the main incident of the day. There were a few scuffles on Easter Road, but we didn't do as well there. At night apparently, Hibs went along to Haymarket on a couple of occasions and there were a few battles. This was becoming normal for a Saturday night.

Despite only getting two points from the previous two games, the team were looking good. It was a settled side that we were turning out, and confidence was growing with each game. We were well up for the next game at Tynecastle, against Rangers, and after an excellent performance, we turned them over 3-0. A great match. More importantly for us, the ICF turned up with a massive firm. Easily 300 lads, and they had a few Chelsea boys with them as well.

The one massive row that I can remember from this game occurred after the match, under the bridge outside the Green Tree pub. The Rangers mob were walking along Gorgie Road as Hearts came out of McLeod Street, and the whole street erupted as the police lost control. I remember one Hearts boy throwing his golf umbrella, javelin style, into the Rangers firm, catching one of their boys full in the face . . . a sore one that must have been. After some pretty heavy fighting, the ICF backed off, but the Chelsea lads stood. There were only about a dozen or so of them, but as Rangers were starting to run, they came piling back into us. Very impressive.

The good run continued for the next two games as we swept past Motherwell 3-0, and Clydebank 4-1 at Tynecastle. This good run had brought us within touching distance of the top of the league. In fact, since Aberdeen didn't have a game, a win away at Dens Park the following Saturday would see us go to the top of the league.

Around 100 of us travelled to Dens Park, and got holed up in a boozer on the outskirts of the city centre. As we left to go to the match, Dundee arrived and there was a bit of a stand off as missiles were thrown by both mobs. The police arrived, steamed in, and everyone scattered. Around ten of us got separated from the main Hearts mob, and as we walked up through Hilltown, a mob of Dundee, about 20 to 30 handed, came piling out of a cafe armed with sauce bottles. We got ran at first, past the Hilltown flats, but eventually we stood and had it, although we took second prize. The game was a bit of a disaster as well. Dundee took an early lead, and Kenny Black missed a penalty for us. However, Ian Jardine snatched a late equaliser for us. So our arrival at the top would have to wait for a bit.

The run up to Christmas saw us draw 1-1 at home to Celtic and win 1-0 away at St Mirren. There were the usual running battles between Hearts and Celtic between the ground and Haymarket station before and after the match, but the most memorable thing about this game was the appearance of a ZULU WARRIORS banner in the away end, presumably held high by some Birmingham City boys.

Christmas was the usual blur of night outs, getting pissed and related festivities. On the Saturday night after the St Mirren game, a few of us went up to a party at Ferniehill. It was a sound piss-up with loads of birds around, but it got well on top afterwards. Three of us were walking up to the main road to head home when a bloke came charging up behind us and pulled a bread knife out of his jacket. Not surprisingly, we scattered. The bloke started running after us, and it was looking well dodgy until we came to a wall which was broken down slightly. Loads of bricks available, we charged back and chased the geezer for ages. Never caught him. Probably just as well. So much for the season of goodwill.

The standards of fashion dipped dramatically during this Christmas. The big thing was tailored jumbo Next cords, or pleated tartan trousers with patent leather shoes, and pastel coloured Sabre knitwear. Sounds disgusting, and looking back, that was probably a fair description.

We had a big match at Ibrox on Saturday, the 28th of December, and everyone was going through. The Friday night before had a few of us deciding to go to Penicuik for a drink. Why, I don't know. It just seemed like a good idea at the time. We ended up in a pub called The Roadhouse. It was packed, and everyone knew everyone else in the pub, except for us. The atmosphere was well heavy right from the start, but all being a bit pissed, we thought fuck it. We stayed in there until around 11pm, and by this time there had been a few stand offs. It was obvious that the locals were waiting for us to leave.

We got out onto the street. All of us had taken bottles out with us, hidden inside our jackets, and we started to walk up to the bus stop. There were about 15 of us, and when the mob piled out the pub after us, they numbered around 30 to 40. They came at us, throwing bottles and glasses. We charged them with our bottles which had them backing off. The Edinburgh bus flew past us as we sprinted back to the bus stop with this whole mob after us. One of our bottles had taken one of their lads out, so they weren't best pleased. Luckily, the bus driver was a sound bloke because he waited for us. If he'd driven away and left us, we'd have been fucked. A scary night, and unfortunately it was to get worse the following day.

Hearts took a huge support through to Ibrox. Around seven to eight thousand in a crowd of 33,000. The CSF had around 150-200 boys, and we done the business in our first encounter with the ICF right outside Queens Street. There was more trouble when we came out of Ibrox underground. The whole street was full of Rangers fans and lads. Hearts charged at them, and had them scattering up the road at first. However, once they regrouped and came back at us, it wasn't too clever. I ended up in a group of about 20 who got separated from the main firm, and we had to get a police escort around to our end. I'll always remember all the Rangers boys flashing their blades, telling us that they were going to cut us on the way home. One Rangers lad basically lent over a copper and smacked me in the face, without the slightest of reactions from the police. When I pointed out what had happened to the policeman, he replied, "You're in Glasgow now, son . . . " Not much you can say to that really.

The game itself was tremendous. Hearts were awesome and two early goals by John Colquhoun were enough to give us our first win at Ibrox since November, 1975. Outside, after the match, was a very different story unfortunately.

We came out the Broomloan shortly before the final whistle and clashed with Rangers behind the main stand as before. This time Rangers had the upper hand and sent Hearts running back down the road. When the police arrived on horses, everyone got a bit mixed up, and while most of the Hearts mob were directed down towards the buses, seven or eight of us ended up walking back to the underground station at Ibrox. We managed to get on the train, but were tumbled when a group of Rangers main lads jumped on our carriage at the next station. We got hammered. The blades came out and one of our lads got slashed up the back of his jacket. I got off lightly, just taking a severe kicking on the floor of the train. What saved us from getting it worse was the fact that the train was so packed. There was barely room to move, but I'll always remember the Stanley blade flashing past my face, about a centimetre away from striping me, before someone floored me with a punch. Luckily, the Rangers firm jumped off at the next station, and we had no more problems all the way back to Edinburgh. I felt like packing the whole thing in there and then, but the fact that we had gone to the top of the league that day ensured that I would carry on.

After the Ibrox ordeal, it was straight back into the deep end with the New Year's Day match against Hibs at Tynecastle. Hibs came down mob handed as usual, but apart from a few small scuffles when the CCS stopped outside the Green Tree Pub, there were no real incidents before the match. Inside the ground, the CCS took up position next to the segregation fence with the Shed, and coins flew back and forth for most of the match. I'll always remember one of the Hibs boys dressed head to toe in Burberry check. Hat, jacket turned inside out so the lining was showing, trousers, brolly. Burberry was at its height at the time, but so much of it on the one body was considered a bit over the top.

After the match the two mobs clashed at the corner of McLeod Street and Gorgie Road. Hibs were about 300 strong and had Hearts backing off down McLeod Street. In other incidents, Hearts and Hibs scarfers clashed, with us getting the better of them on that occasion.

Our next match saw us back through in Motherwell. With us top of the league we had a good sized firm for this match. Easily in excess of 200 boys on the 10.30am through to Queen Street, Glasgow, and we managed to get our revenge on Rangers as soon we came out of the station. They had roughly the same numbers waiting for us, but we charged them out of the station and across George Square. It made me feel a bit better after my ordeal at Ibrox.

The police as usual were on the ball and they soon rounded us up and escorted us to Central for the train to the match, and there was more trouble waiting for us when we arrived in Motherwell. The

Saturday Service charged us as we walked down the road from the station, but we outnumbered them by about two to one, and soon had them on their toes. A great trip so far. The game made it even better as Hearts extended their unbeaten run to 15 games with an easy 3-1 victory.

The main worry for us was the heavy snowfall which at one point looked as if it would get the match abandoned with us coasting to victory. However, the snow abated a bit towards the end of the match, and with some of our closest rivals dropping points, we pulled four points clear at the top.

Despite shit weather all week, over 19,000 turned up at a bitterly cold Tynecastle for the match against one of our main title contenders, Dundee United. Hearts took the lead with a Gary McKay penalty, but United equalised through an Eammon Bannon goal and the game finished 1-1. The only incident of note at this match occurred before the game when around 50 Hearts boys ambushed a similar number of Utility outside Haymarket station. One of the Hearts lads present had a dad who was pretty high up in the Old Bill and he got nicked for smacking a Dundee boy right in front of a police van!

Saturday, the 18th of January, 1986, a totally mammoth day. Aberdeen away. Hearts took over 5,000 fans up to this one and it wasn't a wasted journey with us winning 1-0, John Colquhoun netting with only eight minutes remaining. Hearts had around 250 boys, with the main firm travelling up on two buses, while others made their way on the train or, like me, in transit vans. When the two buses arrived in Aberdeen, they stopped outside the ASC's main boozer, the Schooner Bar. Everyone piled off straight into around 50 Aberdeen lads who disappeared pretty sharpish up the hill, with Hearts in pursuit.

The police then arrived and baton charged Hearts back down the hill, and escorted them to the ground on foot. Our little mob had two transit vans (there was about ten of us in total), and we followed the Portobello bus which also contained a few lads all the way to Aberdeen. On the way, we stopped at Forfar for a drink and a bite to eat. The local mob spotted us, and fronted us up. We leathered them.

Aberdeen had a huge mob inside the ground. Probably around 500, and the missiles were flying over the fence. Two Wolves lads and an Oxford boy came over to introduce themselves inside the ground and they seemed to enjoy their day out with the

Hearts casuals. After the game, the police had it well sorted as they escorted the Hearts mob back to their buses then straight out of town. Just as well really, because the hundreds of Aberdeen boys who were fighting with the police in an attempt to get at us, didn't look as if they were going to mess around.

On the way back, our two vans and the Porty bus stopped off in Perth for about an hour. The Fair City Firm soon sussed us, and they tried to come into a chippy where we were queuing up for some grub before making our way back to our transport. A brief scuffle started at the doorway, and they had quite a few lads, but luckily for us the police arrived and gave us an escort back to the vans and bus.

The Third Round of the Scottish Cup saw just under 28,000 turn up at Tynecastle to witness a memorable 3-2 victory over Rangers. It was a classic Scottish Cup battle, both on and off the pitch. The ICF turned up, over 300 strong, and Hearts had roughly the same, but the police presence was very heavy, and apart from one major off in Dalry Road where hundreds of boys from both sides were fighting before the match, the police managed to contain it for the rest of the day. The game itself was brilliant with Hearts coming from 1-0 down to go 2-1 up midway through the second half. Rangers equalised, and it looked as if the game was going to a replay, when Robertson scored the winner five minutes from time.

Hearts tailed the escorted Rangers mob all the way back to the station, but the police kept the two sides apart. Around 100 Hearts boys started to walk along Shandwick Place into town, when a few Hibs boys were spotted at the West End of Princes Street. Hearts charged and initially the Hibs lads backed off, but when they came charging back, they sent most of the Hearts mob scattering. Embarrassingly, there were only about 25 Hibs lads there. Again, there were a few English lads up for this match. Quite a few from Darlington, two Millwall, and one of Newcastle's top lads.

Leather bloussons were all the rage now, as the out and out designer labels had faded away. Okay, Burberry was still there, but the leathers seemed to be more popular. Thankfully, the Next bubble jackets were history, although Next clothes were still popular. As well as the leather, I bought a Next suede jacket which was very smart. Really soft suede with buttons, it was the business. 101% casual. Things were good with birds at the time as well, as all the girls wanted to go out with a casual. You couldn't fail when the cult was at its peak.

# Chapter Nineteen

February, 1986, began with an away trip to Clydebank again. We took around 150 boys through to this one and the action started at Haymarket Station before we left Edinburgh. Aberdeen were at Ibrox and there were eight ASC lads from Edinburgh and Fife in the station as we arrived. Some of the Muirhouse boys went over to them, and when a kitchen knife was produced, the Aberdeen lads left the station pretty sharpish.

When we arrived in Glasgow there were casuals everywhere. Aberdeen had brought hundreds of lads to Rangers (in excess of 500 apparently), and there were loads of them hanging around the station when we arrived. Thankfully, the police, no doubt mindful of what happened the last time we passed through Glasgow en route to Clydebank, rounded us up and gave us an escort to Central Station. We'd have got a right hiding otherwise, but we still weren't out of the city centre. As we approached Central, the ICF made an appearance, there was a brief scuffle, and the police moved in.

We were then put on the train to Clydebank. As it passed through Partick (I think), we all tried to get off for a beer, but the police on the train prevented this. They grabbed one of my mates, and he turned and looked at the coppers and said, 'You can't nick me cos I'm a Hearts soccer casual!' Priceless.

On arrival at Clydebank, we were put straight into the ground, and there was no further trouble. The game was a bit of a disappointment, although our travelling support of around 4,500 was impressive when you consider that the gate was only 6,000. Anyway, it looked as if our unbeaten run was coming to an end when Sandy Clark popped up to score a late equaliser, although in all honesty this should be looked upon as a point dropped. After the match, we were given a police escort straight back to Edinburgh.

Dundee at home was next and again the Utility made a surprise appearance. Around 150 of them arrived at Haymarket around 2.00pm. There were about 20-30 of us in Dalry Road, and although we stood, we took a bit of a kicking. The police prevented us from getting a right hiding though. There were more Hearts lads on the street nearer the ground, but even still we numbered under 100 on the day.

On the pitch, Hearts done the damage with a comfortable 3-1 win, but the Utility got the result on the street no matter how minor the incident was. With the Dundee clubs going together, they could always catch teams on the hop as you never knew whether they would make an appearance or not, and when they did they normally showed in numbers.

There was no football for a couple of weeks due to our Cup match away at Hamilton getting postponed, but the situation in Edinburgh was getting well on top. Hearts and Hibs lads were clashing almost constantly. Every weekend there were running battles all over the city centre. Lothian Road, Morrison Street, Shandwick Place and Haymarket were regular battlefields. Often the numbers involved were into the hundreds, and the police seemed to be losing control of things. There were also serious incidents between Hibs lads and bouncers at various pubs and clubs. That situation would get a bit heavier in the years to come.

One of the biggest rows between Hearts and Hibs happened on the Saturday night of the postponed Hamilton match. Hearts and some the Rangers Union Jack Bus were drinking together around Haymarket. Hibs turned up mob handed and smashed the windows of a pub, and fighting soon broke out around the area. Even compared to the level of violence of the previous months, this was worse than normal and it would increase the severity of the incidents over the next few weeks which would leave one participant from each side seriously injured.

After our week long break, it was back to Parkhead for a table topping match against Celtic. If anything, this was more lively than our last trip. The headline in the Sunday Mail the following day was 'CASUALS TERROR HITS CITIES', and the story went on to described how over 300 members of the CSF caused havoc in Glasgow, whilst Hibs and Aberdeen casuals fought running battles around the Waverley Station. Another double header of two of Scotland's most violent fixtures.

As we arrived at Queen Street, a massed charge from the train into George Square sent everyone in the area scattering. The police, the Celtic firm, shoppers, students collecting for charity, everyone. The Celtic mob charged back and bottles were flying about everywhere as fighting broke out all over the Square. One of my mates got nicked and he was able to witness the trouble from the back of the police van. He said it looked amazing. There must have been nearer 400 of us and about two to three hundred Celtic. No wonder it took the police ages to control. A few lads from Darlington and Newcastle were again present at this match, along with firms from Kirkcaldy, Livingston, Bathgate, Midlothian, Tranent, Kelso, and the Borders, once again showing how Hearts' hooligan support came largely from the outskirts of Edinburgh and the outlying towns, whereas Hibs were mostly from inner city areas in Edinburgh.

Anyway, eventually the police sorted out an escort, but over 100 of us broke through at Wilson Street when the Celtic mob made an appearance, and we scattered them again. The police called in extra reinforcements to try and contain us, but running battles broke out once more down the London Road. A great day out, particularly when you consider that Robbo managed to snatch an equaliser for us in a 1-1 draw played in front of over 45,000.

The bandwagon in the league was really rolling now, and the team were stringing together some impressive results. However, as our game against St Mirren was postponed the following Saturday, the next match was in the Scottish Cup away at Hamilton on a Monday night. The game was pretty unremarkable, with Hearts winning 2-1. As Hamilton didn't really have any casuals to speak off, there were only about 30-40 Hearts casuals through there, and about half of them had travelled on supporters buses. I had come through on the train with about 20 boys, and as we made our way back to the station, a mob of around 30 Motherwell appeared. They ran us onto the platform, and with nowhere else to go, we fronted it, but unfortunately came off second best, proving the old adage that trouble can come to you when you least expect it.

It was another Cup weekend the following Saturday as well, and with Hibs and Hearts both having home draws, the Hearts - St Mirren match was moved to the Sunday. The Saturday evening saw the continuation of the street battles between Hearts and Hibs from a few weeks previously. Hibs arrived at Haymarket firm handed and in a series of vicious fights, one of their main lads was stabbed, and for a while was quite seriously ill in hospital. Thankfully, he made a full recovery.

The Hibs boys were understandably furious, and a huge mob of them firmed up in Rose Street the following afternoon with the intention of coming down to our match for revenge. The police clocked onto this and moved into disperse a gang of over 100 main Hibs faces. Meanwhile, over at Tynecastle, Hearts romped through to a semi-final tie against Dundee United after easily disposing of a poor St Mirren, 4-1. The LSD had some boys through and there was a series of running battles after the match in Dalry Road, as they were legged back to the station. Most of the trouble came from the Hearts Baby Crew who went on the rampage. The police, in what must have been a busy day for them, arrested 21 Hearts fans, although most were released later without charge.

As well as both Edinburgh teams having Baby Crews at this time, they both had casual mobs of girls, who were not afraid to get stuck in, and were quite prepared to stand and fight alongside the lads. The Hearts girls originally called themselves the Gorgie Ladies Crew, but later changed their name to the Casual Female Firm. They had a few members at their height, although it was only a small hardcore who attended the matches on a regular basis. On the other side of Edinburgh, Hibs had the support of the LST or Ladies Soccer Trendies. Again, they could number quite a few, and also had a hardcore who regularly attended the matches. Like the lads, the girls from both teams dressed fairly similarly, with suede jackets, Lacoste polos, jeans, Burberry scarves, and desert boots or Pod sandals being especially popular.

On the 22nd of March, we had the last derby of the season at Easter Road which we won 2-1, keeping us on course for the league title. The previous week, we had beaten Motherwell 2-0 at home, a game at which no Motherwell boys showed up at. For the Hibs match, over 100 Hearts mobbed up at Haymarket, and walked along Princes Street. There were small mobs of Hibs hanging around, and a few scuffles broke out.

The word got out that we were on our way, and a larger mob of Hibs confronted us in front of The Playhouse, where it went off fairly major, the two mobs standing toe to toe until the police arrived. About eight Hibs and six Hearts were nicked at this incident. After that, the police gave us an escort along London Road and down Easter Road. Once again, there were a few Darlington lads with us, and as we turned into Bothwell Street to go down to the ground, trouble erupted between us and a large group of drunken Hearts scarfers who got the hump when they heard the English accents of the Darlo lads. When the fighting started, hundreds of scarfers got involved, and the police, seeing that we were outnumbered, left them to it. In the end we made a reasonable stand of it, although we did come off second best.

After the match, I was off fairly sharpish as I had to catch a coach through to East Calder for a gig by an English mod band called The Moment. All the bother that we had with East Calder was in the past and it was an excellent gig in front of around 300 mods from all parts of Scotland.

The following Saturday, it was Rangers at home. We had beaten St Mirren 3-0 on the Tuesday at Tynecastle, keeping us out in front, but Celtic, Dundee United and Aberdeen were still keeping the pressure on. Rangers on the other hand were nowhere. Just a mid-table side. It sounds hard to believe nowadays, but this was a match that Hearts were expected to win, and in the end we ran out convincing 3-1 winners with a double from Robbo and a late goal from Sandy Clark. More importantly for us was the level of violence that occurred after the match.

Normally, we left the ground via McLeod Street, but on this occasion we left via Wheatfield Street, signalling to the ICF through the fence that they should turn right on leaving the Gorgie Road End, rather than going towards the station. Once again the mobs were at full strength, with both firms numbering in excess of 300. When you add those numbers to a large amount of Rangers scarfers who were up for it, and a fair percentage of normal Hearts fans who weren't running anywhere, you got chaos. The incidents that erupted after this match have to be some of the most serious ever seen at Tynecastle. Toe to toe fighting involving hundreds of people was eventually broken up by the police, only for both sets of fans to run down to the next connecting street and for the violence to erupt again. This time Rangers backed off a bit, and we ended up having it with them on Gorgie Road. By now it was mostly Rangers scarfers who were up against us, and it was total mayhem. People running across the roofs of stationary cars to get involved, the police being attacked when they tried to nick people, and fighting fans all across Gorgie Road. Mental!

Eventually, the police swamped the area, and charged us up on to Slateford Road, while they got the ICF into an escort to Haymarket, and the Rangers fans to their buses at Chesser. We tried to get at the ICF on Dalry Road, by coming through the underpass from Slateford, but were forced back by the police with dogs, and there were no further incidents that night.

Sweatshirts were big news with the casuals in the spring of '86. Especially if they were by Fiorucci, Best Company, Chipie, and Weekend Warrior. The last one from that list was THE king though. Not least because of the word 'warrior' on each sleeve. Quite fitting for the football casual. Fiorucci was also popular for jeans at this point, and denim jackets. Other popular makes of jeans were Liberto and Armani. A few lads in Edinburgh discovered a small gents outfitters in William Street called Mados. He stocked a lot of obscure Italian labels and they began to be worn too. Also as a Hearts casual newsletter from the time states, clothes by top London fashion houses such as Paul Smith and Katharine Hamnett were beginning to make an appearance inside the football grounds of Scotland.

At the same time, as the casual look became more widespread, cheaper makes such as Jekyll & Hyde (for shirts) enjoyed a little bit of popularity. And again, Next brought out an item that was extremely popular with Edinburgh's casuals. It was a simple white round neck t-shirt, which had a picture of a cricket match on the front, and for a month or so in the spring of '86, it was a must for every self respecting casual in the city.

Calling cards were big news as well. They had hit the front pages originally a few years previously when West Ham stabbed an Arsenal fan to death in London, and scattered cards around his body, and they came back into prominence after Millwall fans ran amok at a service station, slashing an opposing fan. The card left at that incident, bearing the legend, 'CONGRATULATIONS, YOU HAVE JUST MET MILLWALL!' appeared in many of the tabloids. Within days, the papers were full of cards from the Chelsea Headhunters, Portsmouth 6:57 Crew, and a Hearts one, as the media milked the latest soccer outrage. The Hearts card that made the press was a very basic photocopied effort, but we actually had proper colour cards made, giving us one of the best calling cards in Britain.

The general public were shocked at the appearance of those cards. Not surprising really, as the thought of scattering cards around the body of a battered victim is a bit sick. However, while I can't say that this didn't happen, the vast majority of the cards were left in pub toilets in towns, on buses, trains, and so on, and were used to wind people up. Let's face it, you didn't really want to take a calling card to a game with you. Imagine if you got nicked with that in your possession. Bang goes your defence of just walking up the road minding your own business, when suddenly you got caught up in trouble! They were evidence of your involvement in organised football violence, and invited the courts to throw the book at you.

* * *

Scottish Cup semi-final day provided a welcome break from the rigours of the league campaign, as we travelled to Hampden Park for the first of two successive matches against Dundee United. With Hibs playing Aberdeen in the other semi-final at Dens Park, the talk in Edinburgh in the week leading up to the two big games was of an all Edinburgh final. Unfortunately, this wasn't to be with Aberdeen winning a match that was more memorable for the violence before and after on the streets of Dundee, as Scotland's big two clashed. We had a good travelling support in excess of 20,000 to cheer us onto a 1-0 victory courtesy of a Colquhoun goal (not bad when you consider that the crowd was just under 31,000). There were around 200 casuals amongst our support and although there was no trouble with the Dundee United firm, we had a good battle with Celtic outside Central Station before the match which finished about honours even, with quite a few arrested from both sides.

Part two of the Dundee United double header was at Tannadice in a vital league match on the 12th of April. United had beaten Aberdeen in midweek and a win against us would've kept them in the title race. A capacity crowd of around 22,500, including about 7,000 Hearts, watched us coast to a 3-0 win with one of our best performances in years. Robertson the hero once again with two excellent goals.

There was another great turnout of Hearts boys for this game, around 300 of us. The whole mob travelled up together on the train, and were able to have a drink in Dundee and walk up to the ground untroubled. On arrival at the ground, their firm who also numbered hundreds, made an appearance outside the main stand. Hearts charged them and running battles broke out along the street. The United firm ended up getting run, but one of their lads was caught and took quite a serious beating before the police moved in to break things up.

As the dust settled, there were two lads in our midst who nobody recognised. We thought that they were a couple of Utility lads being a bit wide, and pulled them up. They turned out to be two of Manchester United boys, one of whom, still follows Hearts. After the match, the two lads came with us, and when it went off on the way back to the station they got involved straight away. A good away win on and off the pitch.

The run-in for the league title had started. We only needed four points from our last three games to claim our first Scottish Championship since 1960. We were at home to Aberdeen and

Clydebank, and away to Dundee. Now, we all blame the result at Dundee for losing the league, but as far as I'm concerned we chucked it away against Aberdeen.

The game had been moved to a Sunday, an event that I always feel ruins the atmosphere. Even with just under 20,000 inside the ground and Hearts dividing the Gorgie Road End terrace in half so that we could use it, the atmosphere was very subdued. It might have been nerves that kept such a bumper crowd quiet, but if so, then we must take responsibility for the result, because that day, of all days, we should've got right behind the team.

Aberdeen were out of the race completely, after a promising season as defending champions had finished poorly. Alex Ferguson and Aberdeen were finding out the hard way that you couldn't manage a club side and the international team simultaneously without some dropping of standards (Fergie was brought in as the caretaker manager of Scotland for the Mexico '86 World Cup campaign after Jock Stein's sudden death at Ninian Park).

Anyway, Aberdeen were the more composed team as Hearts were very jittery, and the Dons took the lead with only 18 minutes left through a hotly disputed penalty given for hand ball. It wasn't in doubt that Ian Jardine handled the ball, but Jim Bett had also handled it a second before. Unfortunately, the referee, Bob Valentine, must have missed that one. Hearts battled back, and indeed played a lot better after going 1-0 down, and equalised with just a few minutes left on the clock. Some of you may see it as a point gained with the last gasp equaliser, but this was a home game, and I feel that this was the game that we missed our chance.

There wasn't much trouble at this match. With Aberdeen having nothing to play for, they hadn't really travelled, and their mob was only around 30 strong. There was a brief altercation as the Aberdeen lads were escorted into Haymarket Station, but nothing of any note.

We won our next home match 1-0 against Clydebank in front of over 20,000. There were loads of Hearts lads at this match, as a good sunny day heralded a big drinking session. Once again nerves affected the team - an omen which wasn't good for a title race that was going to the wire. Again, this was another wasted opportunity at home as we could and should have boosted our goal difference a bit here, although the more cynical amongst you may suggest that no matter how big our goal difference, Celtic would still have got the required number of goals against St Mirren in their final game!

Saturday, the 3rd of May, 1986. A date that will haunt Hearts fans forever more. Just in case there is anyone reading this who is not aware of the facts, here's a quick recap. The championship going into the final weekend was a two horse race between Hearts and Celtic. We were away at Dundee and the Celts were away at St Mirren. Hearts were two points clear (when you got two points for a win) with a goal difference advantage of four. Putting it down on paper like this, it seems hard to see how we managed to chuck it away, but anything is possible with Hearts. The fact that an Edinburgh official, Bill Crombie, was refereeing the match at Dundee would seem to be another thing in our favour, although in reality this was not to be, as he refused us an early stonewall penalty, later admitting that he was wrong.

Anyway, thousands of Hearts fans (an estimated 10,000 in a crowd of 19,500) travelled to Dundee in a party mood. The way some people were carrying on, it was like a foregone conclusion that we would win, a sentiment that I didn't share. Years of following Hearts as a youngster has taught me never to make assumptions. The fans were certainly more confident than the team were, not least because the players had been decimated by a flu outbreak in the week leading up to the match. In hindsight the club should probably have tried to get this match postponed.

I can't say for certain how many CSF were at this match, as there were large mobs on many different trains, but there were hundreds of us. From the Borders to West and East Lothian, from Fife to Edinburgh, every Hearts casual travelled to this one. At a rough guess, I'd say there were about 500 Hearts boys at this game. I travelled up in a mob of around 30 strong on a train getting into Dundee for opening time. After a few hours in the pub, we made our way to the ground and entered without any problems. We had barely seen a Dundee fan, let alone one of their lads.

The atmosphere was electric inside the ground, and whilst I won't comment too much on the game, Hearts did start off quite promisingly, creating a few good chances, and as mentioned before, being denied a definite penalty. However, at half-time the mood amongst the crowd began to change when it was announced that Celtic were 4-0 up against St Mirren. This got worse as news came over just after the restart that they had increased their lead to 5-0. Panic set in, and despite a few tactical changes to the team to try to hold out for the draw, Dundee were coming more into the match. With only seven minutes left, Albert Kidd opened the scoring for

Dundee. The Hearts players and fans could hardly comprehend what was happening.

Half the team were visibly struggling with the pace, the effects of the flu bug taking their toll, and despite an attempt at a fight back, Albert Kidd struck again with only three minutes left. Immediately after this goal, hundreds of Hearts lads and fans spilled over onto the pitch and charged across to the Dundee covered terrace. They didn't want to know, and made no attempt to come onto the pitch. The police realising the volatility of the situation, played it low profile, and rather than trying to arrest the invaders, they just cleared the pitch.

As the final whistle went, there was stunned disbelief amongst the Hearts fans and team, and more fans spilled onto the park. We all left right on the final whistle and went mental. As the Hearts fans cried inside the ground, the CSF ran amok outside. Can't really say much more about this apart from Dundee trashed, city and people.

Although we still had the Cup Final against Aberdeen to look forward to, as far as I was concerned that was the season over. We knew that the bubble had burst, and held no expectations for this match. The week leading up to the match was a nightmare, as half of Edinburgh found our 2-0 defeat at Dundee highly amusing. I suppose you have to find amusement somewhere, and if the boot had been on the other foot, what Hearts fan would've acted any differently?

Anyway, I had a ticket, and although still sickened with the way things had gone in the league, I and 40,000 other Hearts fans travelled through to Hampden, clutching at that last bit of hope that we could salvage something from the season. As the crowd was only 62,800, once again Hearts had the majority of the support, making a mockery of the claim from Aberdeen that they are Scotland's third largest team. They aren't even fourth, as I would put Hibs above Aberdeen in terms of the size of potential support.

Once again there was an excellent turnout of casuals, almost as many as we had the previous week. A lot came up from England for this match from Darlington, Newcastle, Millwall, and Chelsea, amongst others. Aberdeen had a huge mob that day as well, easily matching us. Most of us were in the section next to the ASC during the match. They were all standing down the front behind a Union Jack with A/DEEN TRENDIES (I think) on it. There was loads of verbal from both sides during the match with an almost constant exchange of missiles over the fence.

On the pitch, Aberdeen's big game experience was evident and Hearts were well beaten 3-0 in the end. Luck had deserted us completely, with yet another penalty appeal turned down, and Walter Kidd being sent off.

Once again there was mayhem after the match as large mobs clashed. Memorable incidents saw around 100 Aberdeen charging down a hill at Hearts and being battered by Hearts casuals and regular fans alike, an Aberdeen fan wearing a Cup Final top hat getting a smack (he deserved it for wearing such a stupid hat), and a brilliant clash between around 50 Hearts and 25 Aberdeen - no running, no backing off, no weapons, just toe to toe punch for punch. Respect to both sides.

The '85-'86 season had everything apart from the silverware that the team and the fans deserved. Good mobs, good clothes (some of the time), and some brilliant days out.

# Conclusion

The '85/'86 season witnessed the height of the casual movement in Scotland in my view. From then on, the police gradually began to get things sussed. As a result the gangs got better organised, but smaller. A hardcore remained, but a lot of people dropped out as the level of violence escalated.

Although I still watched Hearts regularly, and carried on with wearing the latest labels, I began to drift away from being involved. I have stopped at the end of that season because I am unable to give first hand accounts of many of the incidents that happened in future seasons. Travelling to away games on a supporters bus from my local pub became my preferred method of transport to aways, arriving early in towns so we could get a few beers down before the match. As a result of this, there were occasions when trouble broke out which was fair enough. I just didn't want to go looking for it anymore.

Anyway, as the violence escalated with weapons being used, it got too heavy for me. The fact that I still enjoyed the fashion aspect of the casual movement though meant that I wasn't able to entirely escape from the trouble altogether, especially in the city centre where Hearts and Hibs were having street battles on an almost weekly basis now. As a lot of people got involved for purely the violence, the labels seemed to become less important for some. Before it had as much to do with looking better than the opposing mob as actually turning them over, but latterly all that mattered was the violence. Yeah, sure there were tear ups before, but a mob could lose as much face if one of your numbers was spotted wearing last month's trainers by the opposition's fashion police, as it would being on their toes at Pittodrie, Ibrox, Easter Road, or wherever.

I was never a serious football rucker, just someone (like so many others) who went along for a laugh and to make up the numbers. As the numbers fell, the firms actually got more violent as only the hardcore were left. Putting on a show for a few minutes directly outside or inside a ground or in a city centre was what I was into, not organised meets in back streets miles away from the stadiums. That was for the serious players only and I knew my limitations.

Priorities also change, and the incoming club scene, soul Allnighters, and speeding out your nut at Caister and Camber Sands

Weekenders became preferable to meeting someone's "Uncle Stanley" on the Glasgow underground. I was still bang into football, and still took an interest in the hooligan scene from a distance, but other interests took over. Then a mortgage and a wife and all the resulting responsibilities mean that you have too much to lose by getting nicked at the football. Especially nowadays, when the authorities reaction is often out of all proportion to the severity of your offence. Punch someone in a pub, and if it even gets to court, you're looking at a £200 fine tops. Do it at a football match and suddenly it becomes worthy of a £500 plus fine or even imprisonment. Where's the justice in that?

Anyway, a brief overview of the highlights watching Hearts in the years from 1986 has to centre around the European aways, especially when we almost (if we had taken that late chance in the Olympic Stadium, Munich) got to a semi-final with Napoli in the UEFA Cup. However, one point to make about that Cup run was the appearance of the bandwagon jumpers and their intolerance in Munich. In Vienna, there were only about six or seven hundred Hearts fans in attendance, with around ten Union Jacks in the Hearts end. And we ran the Austrian firm through the woods and the fun fair after the match. In Mostar there were around 200 of us, and again Union Jacks were being flown as fires were set on the terraces. The paramilitary Serbian police force had to escort us to our buses because literally thousands of Bosnians tried to attack us. Around 30 of us steamed into hundreds of them at one point. Superb.

Then a glamour game in Munich sees about 4,000 Hearts fans turning up, and all of a sudden there's people moaning about the Union Jacks and the SFA official instructing us to take them down. Bet they never asked Rangers to do that.

Other great Euro trips were Prague for the Dukla match when it was still a Communist country, and the tourists hadn't rediscovered it yet. Bottles of Budvar lager for around 5p. Paradise. Liege where around 200 of the infamous Hell Side gang of Standard Liege were ran ragged by around 30 Hearts boys. Unfortunately, I didn't see that one first hand, but actually heard about that incident in a pub in central Liege where Hearts fans were loudly condemning the action of the Hearts mob for "giving us a bad name" and all that bollocks. Maybe they should come into the real world. Do they really think that the Hell-Side Boys had got 200 of their lads together for no reason? They were looking for trouble, and if the casuals hadn't put themselves up for it, they would have started on whatever groups of Hearts fans they could find.

The late Eighties also saw alliances between the gangs following Scottish clubs and their counterparts in England. The most widely publicised of those link ups was between the ICF gang at Rangers and the Chelsea Headhunters. In fact, it wasn't just the gangs that were involved in this friendship. It seemed to be the support in general after they got on well together when Chelsea played Rangers at Stamford Bridge in a friendly match to raise money for the Bradford Fire Disaster Benefit. Aberdeen had links with Leeds for a while, and latterly with Tottenham, Celtic's fans and Manchester United supporters have always got on well, and Dundee United seem to have linked up with Stoke City after a chance meeting between some of the lads while on holiday abroad.

At Hearts, as mentioned earlier, lads from the Bank Top 200 gang at Darlington and the 6:57 Crew at Portsmouth were early regular visitors to Hearts games. I'll always remember a game against Celtic at Tynecastle in the late Eighties when a large group of Pompey had come up. Instead of leaving from the usual McLeod Street exit, we left from the Wheatfield exit, and walked right through thousands of Celtic fans making their way back to their buses. There were about 50 of us in total and we kicked it off with them. It looked as if we'd get killed, but when we charged they backed off. It was like the parting of the Red Sea as we charged through them. When we got to the other side of the Gorgie Road End exit, a few of the Pompey lads looked visibly shaken. I didn't blame them.

Then there was the friendly away at Airdrie when Hearts won 5-0. A Hearts / Pompey firm numbering around 25 lads went into the Airdrie end and scattered them by using CS gas. As well as the friendships with Darlington and Portsmouth, Manchester City and Hearts fans in general seem to have a bit of a friendship.

Hibs were never really into teaming up with English mobs, adopting a we hate everyone approach. However, they were friendly with the FYC (Fine Young Casuals) for a while who follow Oldham Athletic. That was until Hibs played down in Oldham in a friendly, and decided to kick it off. Continuing a fine tradition for Edinburgh teams kicking it off in Oldham, as Hearts took the Chaddy End in September, '74, during a Texaco Cup match, as confirmed by Carl H Spiers in his excellent book about Oldham thugs, *We Are The Famous Football Hooligans*.

Hibs always seemed to get good pre-season friendlies. As well as their away game in Oldham, they had a match at Villa Park where they kicked it off with Birmingham City lads near New Street Station, then ran Villa at the ground. However, their highlight was going down to The Den for a match with Millwall, and running amok down the Old Kent Road on a Friday night. A formidable task at the best of times, even if Millwall hadn't been playing.

Hearts on the other hand never really got any good English sides away. There was Watford for a testimonial, and a good mob travelled, but no trouble. The most memorable thing about that game was the huge drunken conga. We took a few to the Baseball Ground for a match against Derby, but again no real problems.

However, all the experiences pale into insignificance when compared to the Scottish Cup win. Quite simply my greatest moment, and that is all I can say. I've not got the literary skills to put down on paper how I felt that day. Watching my hometown team win a major honour was a dream come true. That last sentence sums it up, especially the word "hometown". That's what it was all about, supporting your hometown team. I can't understand people from Edinburgh, Motherwell, Aberdeen, and elsewhere who support the Old Firm instead of their local side.

Where do we go from here? Despite the elation of our Cup win, football is finished. It has lost all sense of reality. It has ditched its working class roots at the higher level in both Scotland and England, and it's pricing the genuine fans out of the game and replacing them with corporate hospitality. I'm glad that Hearts have finally won something because now I can walk away from the game with that memory. I still love football at its grassroots level, but I want no part in the corporate entertainment package that it has now become. The nouveau fan has won. It's their game now. Let's just hope that they remain loyal to the game when football becomes unfashionable again.

Well, I hope you have enjoyed my insight into the Edinburgh football scene during the early to mid Eighties. I wasn't sure about writing it, but thought that I'd put something down on paper now that it's all behind me. It would be better if one of the major players at Hearts, or at Hibs for that matter, had written it rather than just one of the followers, but maybe that will eventually happen. In the meantime, hopefully this will fill a gap in Edinburgh's local social history section in the library.

It would be great if in the future someone put together a book about following Hearts in the Seventies. The true golden age of football hooliganism. Also, something covering the Edinburgh street gang scene of the Seventies when you had The Young Leith Team, Young Gillie Team, Young Mental Drylaw and the rest. It would be good to read your stories, and there is definitely a market for that type of book. Only those who were there can present things how they really happened, and if nobody bothers, it is left to the media's interpretation of events as far as the history books are concerned, which rarely tells the full story.

The Seventies and Eighties were violent eras, and very gang orientated. Do I have any regrets about it all? The answer has to be no. It was part of our culture, it was exciting, and I wouldn't have missed it for the world. The casual movement was and is widely derided by countless clueless commentators, but you only need to look around any city centre pub on a Saturday night to see the massive impact that the casuals have had on contemporary British menswear. We totally revolutionised fashion for men in this country. The middle class 'experts' on youth culture and the media will try to dismiss the casuals as no more than thugs, but it is us who took the designer labels off the catwalks and onto the terraces. Before we came along, your Saturday night crowd would be kitted out in Burton's finest, but now there are labels everywhere. All the lads who were in on it from the start know that the casuals represented far too important a movement to be dismissed as yob culture.

Times may have changed, but one thing remains constant. The memories of days gone by, following the Hearts home and way. Bring out your riot gear - Hearts are here!

"Meanwhile, in Glasgow shoppers fled in
terror as Hearts' Casuals ran amok.  More
than 300 members of the CSF - Hearts'
Capital Soccer Firm - arrived in Glasgow
for the Premier League clash against
Celtic.  Seconds after leaving the train
at Queen Street Station they were wreaking
havoc.  A mass charge into George Square
was followed by fights and
bottle-throwing."

Sunday Mail, 1985

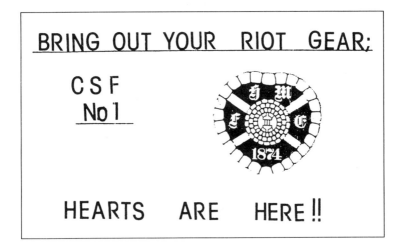

congratulations
you've just met
**HEARTS**
pride
of
SCOTLAND
A ... PRODUCTION

# HEARTS
# SOCCER SAVAGES

WHO WANTS TO KNOW?

CSF Production

HEARTS CSF

WE ARE THE FIRM

"Hearts directors are seeking talks with
the police in a bid to stamp out football
hooliganism - after a night in which up to
1000 fans went on the rampage.  The fans,
mainly Hearts' supporters, left a trail of
destruction in Edinburgh from Easter Road
to Princes Street after last night's
Hibs-Hearts derby . . . Mr John Frame,
secretary of the Federation Of Hearts
Supporters' Clubs said, 'These
troublemakers used to be a minority, but
that is not the case now' . . . "

                    Edinburgh Evening Post, 1982

THE VOICE OF HEARTS YOUTH

## C.S.F. SOCCER TRENDIES
### OFFICIAL NEWSLETTER

### TYNECASTLE TOPICS

Well since the last Newsletter we have seen HEARTS go to the top of the League, Football, violence and style wise. No-on can dispute the fact that the HEARTS YOUTH are the hardest and smartest mob of trendy youths in the country, and this will be proved beyond doubt after we do HIBS in a couple of weeks time. We have already smashed MOTHERWELL, RANGERS, CELTIC and the tramps (ABERDEEN) who are the only other worthwhile crews and HIBS are next to fall. What we've got up our sleeves for them is different class. This could be the BIG one.

Media publicity has also increased dramtically in our favour after smashing CELTIC and overall the incidents with the Calling Cards which were incidentally ones made up by the BABY CREW and are not the genuine article. (Why not have a whip round and get money to have proper ones printed on Card).

### HAMILTON v HEARTS

Quite a disappointing turnout for this one after the big crews we've had for recent games (400 approx. v Celtic) only 50 of us, but still nobody dared to mess with the HEARTS CASUALS. MOTHERWELL'S crew the SATURDAY SHITTERS lived up to their name by not daring to come near us, after threats of violence even although they outnumbered us 2 - 1. Well we've just got one thing to say to MOTHERWELL and that is, if you want to ruck we'll see you at TYNECASTLE if you dare, and something for HAMILTON'S crew is, if you get promoted to the Premier League don't even bother about having a CASUAL CREW because people under 12 years who wear clothes similar to ABERDEEN e.g. Kappa, Nike, Bleached Jeans etc get slagged by the rest of us. For instance we are getting into the Italian Designer gear stocked by Mario's or the products of top LONDON Designers like PAUL SMITH, STEPHEN KING, KATHERINE HAMNETT etc.

### FORTHCOMING FIXTURES

Quite a boring Fixture List till the end of the Season, the only highspots being when we have HIBS at Easter Road and if ABERDEEN dare to bring a Crew down to TYNECASTLE because they shit it the last time. We will no doubt get some running practice when we chase RANGERS and it will be interesting to see if the "FAMOUS?" Love Street Division do actually exist. Only two more away matches left and that's to DUNDEE twice which is very boring. At least we don't have to go back to TOUGH Glasgow (HA! HA!) and chase small boys about who think it's hard to throw bottles.

---

**P.S.** Hello to our English counterparts who are taking an interest in us - DARLINGTON, CHELSEA, MILLWALL, MANCHESTER CITY and NEWCASTLE. You are welcome to TYNECASTLE anytime.

---

**P.P.S.** HEARTS girls have changed their name from GLC to CFF (Casual Female Firm). They have about 30 Members (all good-lookers as well)

---

Well that's all for now and remember keeping HEARTS top lies with you. NO SURRENDER! C.S.F. HEARTS F.C.

136

"Hearts supremo Wallace Mercer was
'astonished' when he came face-to-face
with a football lout.  For he was a well
spoken civil servant who works as a
taxman.  And Mercer was dumbfounded to
find that the fan identified as ringleader
of a hooligan gang was married, smartly
dressed and well groomed."

The Sun, 1985

"There is on exhibition at the ground a
hard ball of elastic bands (bigger than a
cricket ball) with a stone in the middle.
Police lifted lumps of concrete the size
of your fist and there were innumerable
coins . . . all from the Hearts end. Alex
Macdonald and Sandy Jardine should have
been beaming at their 2-1 win . . . but
they were shocked by the conduct of their
own supporters in the 18,000 crowd. 'It
was scandalous,' said Sandy. 'The
atmosphere was far worse than anything
Alex or I experienced in games between
Celtic and Rangers. What do they expect
to achieve by running onto the pitch? If
they can't take it when we lose a goal,
then they out to stay away.' . . . "

The Edinburgh Evening Post, 1984

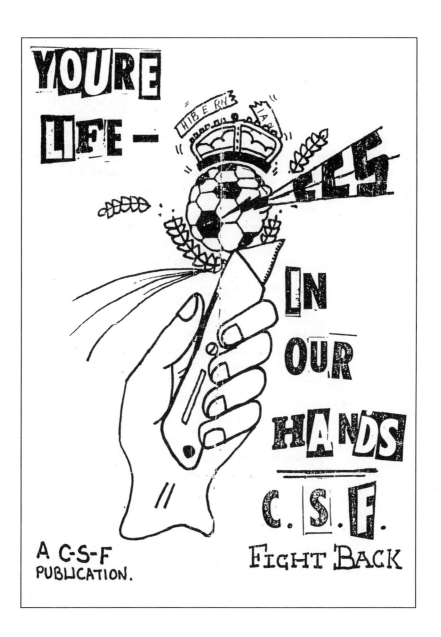

## SUNDAY POST ARTICLE

Well you will probably have heard how untrendy we are in the Fashions compared to other Clubs. This is RUBBISH, compared to HIBS (Capital City Scruffs) etc, We are the best dressed except for maybe ABERDEEN. It has, however been noted that some of the Hearts Baby Crew have been steadily declining into being scruffs, so either get a grip lads or stop coming with us. Congratulations however for appearance go to our ever growing contingent of female members. They have formed the G.L.C. (Gorgie Ladies Crew) and seem quite well organised. Keep up the good work girls.

HEARTS v ABERDEEN - Lets show this bunch of saps that brotherly love (Sunday Post) can quickly turn into hate with a big turnout and a good showing in the fighting with Aberdeen. We've done them before and we'll do it again. Some of us will be boarding Aberdeen's train at Kirkcaldy, so we're relying on you for reinforcements to spring the usual ambush at Haymarket.

OPERATION LOCOMOTION - We have been asked by both Motherwell and Aberdeen to join up with them for Scottish Casuals big day. They just have to be joking. There's no way that Hearts (so obviously Scotland's number ones now) would joint up with any of that lot of bottlers. We all know who, we ourselves play on that day so that could be another Flash-point for the Press to glorify and get totally wrong. (More information in next Bulletin available at the Aberdeen Match).

P.S. To all Clubs in England especially our counterparts Millwall & Chelsea keep up the good work.

"What a pity that a memorial game to Tom
Hart at Easter Road was turned into a hate
game by louts who masquerade as supporters
of Hearts . . . because Hibs had the
temerity to beat them.  About 5,000 of
those who go to Tynecastle are hooligans
whose parents should give them a damn good
walloping and save everyone else a lot of
trouble."

Shoot Magazine, 1982

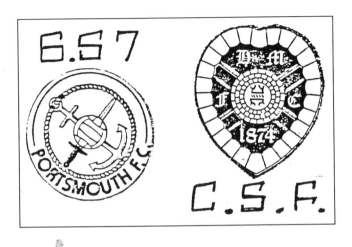

"Three policemen were in hospital with
head injuries last night after a battle
broke out among Hearts fans.  The trouble
started when the home side went down 1-0
to Motherwell at Tynecastle.  Fighting
flared in the first half shortly after
Motherwell scored the only goal in this
vital league decider.  A policeman was
struck on the head as he tried to make an
arrest . . . Police arrived in force but
another two officers received head
injuries and all three were taken to
hospital for treatment . . ."
Edinburgh Evening News, 1982

# Come ahead if you think you're hard enough . . .

Terrace Banter was launched in October, 1998, as a football imprint of S.T. Publishing. Over the past decade football as a spectator sport has changed beyond all recognition, particularly for the ordinary fan. A great deal of working class culture and tradition is being cast to one side so that football can appeal to a new market, that of the "soccer fan".

Through Terrace Banter we hope to put down in print the experiences of the ordinary fan before they are lost forever in a sea of plastic seats and replica strips. Unless we document our own history, it is left to outsiders and the mass media to be judge and jury.

This book is primarily about Hearts hooligans, but it is also about growing up on the terraces. We are interested in hearing from other firms, both in Scotland and elsewhere, who would like to publish a book about their exploits. Each book would represent a piece in a jigsaw puzzle, and together would give as good a picture of what really happened as you're likely to find.

Even if you don't think you could write the book yourself, we can help you get your words into print.


You can write to us at

Terrace Banter
P.O. Box 12
Lockerbie
DG11 3BW
Scotland

# Other books from
# Terrace Banter and S.T. Publishing

### SATURDAY'S HEROES by Joe Mitchell
### Price £3.95
It's all right for the mugs in their executive boxes and expensive seats to moan about football hooliganism. They've never had to defend their end against rival fans or fight their way back to a train station after an away game. But Paul West and his skinhead crew don't care what others think of them anyway. They live in a violent world that sees them do battle with casual gangs, other skinheads and rival supporters. A world that is slowly torn apart by aggro, a certain girl, and betrayal.

### CASUAL by Gavin Anderson
### Price £5.99
"The mob swayed towards the already rocking fence and buckling gates. The police constables looked on in horror as hundreds of hooligans crushed onto the side of the pens. A few of the coppers were already radioing for assistance, and when the higher ranking officers saw what was happening, they immediately ordered the gates to be unlocked. The ghost of Hillsborough still haunted them. The Chelsea firm burst through and shoved past the police and straight into the Red Army. A flare was fired from the Chelsea mob into the tightly packed opposition, instantly scattering them in all directions. The air was thick with bricks and bottles as running battles filled the street . . . "

### AND UP STEPS MICHAEL GRAY -
### The Secret Diary Of A Sunderland Fan Aged 28¾
### Price £9.99
224 page book that takes you on a rollercoaster ride through the 1997-98 season that began at the Stadium Of Light and ended so cruelly at Wembley Stadium. It's all here. The ups and downs of a season that had us on the edges of our spanking new seats, the away days, the joys of radio when you can't get a ticket, the hatred of Newcastle, ventures into the chemical wastelands to play Boro, facing the Mag at work come Monday morning . . .

### SINGIN' THE BLUES by Neil Nixon
### Price £9.99
One man, one team, one love. Neil Nixon started supporting Carlisle United as a boy. Years later, he's still there. This is his story.
> "Excellent, bloody excellent . . . By turns, hilarious, tragic and chillingly honest. This may well be the best book about one man and his team since Fever Pitch."
> **STEVEN WELLS, NME**

**The above books are available from all good bookshops or by post from STP MAIL ORDER, P.O. Box 12, Lockerbie. DG11 3BW. Make cheques payable to STP Mail Order. There is nothing to add for postage and packing.**